Watch Me Ju

Watch Me Jumpstart is a love letter and a jab to the ribs—part memoir, part field guide—from the Artistic Director who spent three decades peering behind the curtain of the Ottawa International Animation Festival. Chris Robinson has watched the medium mutate from spliced film cans and ¾-inch tapes to links and torrents of digital files; from a handful of global showcases to a crowded calendar of festivals; and from outsider, DIY voices to an industry that can smooth every rough edge—and sometimes sand away the soul.

With his trademark dry bite and disarming honesty, Robinson traces the collisions that shaped his life in animation: the punky spirit that got him hired, the near-disasters that almost sank him, the programmes that soared, and the friendships forged at 2 a.m. over cheap wine and weirder shorts. He doesn't romanticize the past or panic about the future; he simply records what it feels like to stand at the crossroads—again and again—while the art form reinvents itself and argues for the stubborn, personal, beautifully impractical films that keep the medium alive.

Watch Me Jumpstart is for animators and students, for programmers and critics, and for anyone who ever fell for a film that didn't care about permission. It's a backstage pass to the decisions, arguments, and small miracles that turn thousands of submissions into a festival—and a reminder that animation isn't a genre or a market segment. It's a messy, human conversation that never stops moving, even when the projector jams.

Chris Robinson is a Canadian writer and the Artistic Director of the Ottawa International Animation Festival (OIAF). A leading figure in the animation world, Robinson has received several prestigious honours, including the *Animafest Zagreb Award for Outstanding Contribution to Animation Studies* (2020) and the *Prix René Jodoin* (2022) for his contributions to Canadian animation. Widely regarded as "one of the most stylistically original and provocative experts in the history of animation," Robinson's influence extends across writing, curation, and film.

He first gained attention through his eclectic and influential magazine column, *Animation Pimp*, which was later adapted into a book of the same name. His most recent animation writing includes *Earmarked for Collision*, the first ever history of collage animation. His other animation books include *Dreaming a way (of) Life*, a book about the legendary collage filmmaker, Lewis Klahr, and *Raw Outrage: The Films of Phil Mulloy.*

In addition to his writing on animation, he also wrote the award-winning animated short, *Lipsett Diaries* (2010), directed by Theodore Ushev. He recently completed the illustrated novel *My Balls Are Killing Me* with artist Andreas Hykade and wrote the script for the live action feature, *Idling*, directed by Theodore Ushev.

Watch Me Jumpstart

Strutting and Stumbling Through Animation

Chris Robinson

CRC Press
Taylor & Francis Group
Boca Raton London New York

CRC Press is an imprint of the
Taylor & Francis Group, an **informa** business

Designed cover image: Phil Mulloy

First edition published 2027
by CRC Press
2385 NW Executive Center Drive, Suite 320, Boca Raton FL 33431

and by CRC Press
4 Park Square, Milton Park, Abingdon, Oxon, OX14 4RN

CRC Press is an imprint of Taylor & Francis Group, LLC

ISBN: 9781041059684 (hbk)
ISBN: 9781041059660 (pbk)
ISBN: 9781003633181 (ebk)

DOI: 10.1201/9781003633181

Typeset in Minion
by codeMantra

Watch me jumpstart as the old skin is peeled
See an opening and bust into the field
Hidden longings no longer concealed
Watch me bulldoze every bulldozer away
Each new obstacle from each old new day
Where it's going it's hard for me to say

"Watch Me Jumpstart" lyrics by Robert
Pollard (performed by Guided by Voices)

For Kelly Neall, the unsung hero of the OIAF. Without her, there's no OIAF and I'd be working in a parking garage.

Contents

Introduction

So, what is this?

Good question.

I'm not entirely sure. Maybe by the time I finish writing, I'll know. Maybe by the time you finish reading, you'll know. Let's find out.

Honestly, this began in spite—sparked by the barely sober charlatans littering the animation festival landscape. But spite alone doesn't justify the inane slog of writing. In 35 years with the Ottawa International Animation Festival (OIAF), I've watched the ground shift: thousands more films a year; longer, more personal work; sharper technique; broader voices. More schools. More students. More studios. Way more festivals. If the landscape was sparse in 1991, it's overpopulated in 2026.

Festivals are essential to this community. They're not just launchpads—they're bridges, temporary spaces where people from around the world connect. They link films to audiences, filmmakers to each other, and stories to new possibilities. They're where deals are made, teams are built, and sometimes whole careers begin. It's also where friendships are born—often not in screening rooms but in local bars and assorted festival parties. Social events are as important as the screenings.

Despite all the personal, technical, and national histories animation holds, we rarely hear from the people behind the scenes—festival programmers and organizers. Not because we're more important but because we watch thousands of films a year. That's a perspective few others in the animation community have—or want. I've seen bits and pieces of hundreds of thousands of films. That exposure changes how you see the medium. It's a rare privilege (though sometimes it feels like punishment): looking out over this vast animation landscape and seeing and hearing all these different visions and voices. It's maybe why I can be a bit harsher toward films than some. I know I'm seen as a bit aloof and

DOI: 10.1201/9781003633181-1

even teetering toward rude or cruel. Part of that is that I'm not a naturally social person, and also part of it is because I come to animation from a very different world (as you will see), but mostly I'd argue it's because I have this window into animated films few others have. Again, I'm not saying I am so damn special, just that I have a different perspective than any animator does.

This isn't a personal memoir, exactly—though my writing always ends up somewhere between personal reflection, history, and fiction. What follows is my account of what I've witnessed in animation, how the community evolved, and what's been lost or gained along the way. I'm not here to mourn or celebrate change. Change just is.I'd call this a fragmented recollection of a life in animation. This could have been an Animation Confidential tell-all about scandals, wild times, and misbehaviours, but, well, there is some of that because we're humans, we make decisions, good and bad, and all that should be part of the story.

I guess what I really wanted was to leave a document, a first-person perspective on a time and a scene now passing. Maybe it gives younger generations a sense of how things worked before. We tend to race from festival to festival without pausing to look back. But we have to. We need the past to understand where we are—and, maybe, where we're headed. This is a record of what it felt like to be in animation through several eras. In 1995, I was the youngest—or one of the youngest—animation festival directors. Today, I am—as is, I believe, my comrade-in-arms, Kelly Neall—one of the longest-serving animation-festival directors. So, I've seen a lot during what has been a transformative period in animation.

It's not just the festival side. I've had a pretty decent career as a writer and author of books on animation. Writing helped me understand this world and led me to highlight overlooked artists—those whose work has too often gone unseen by both the public and the art world. I've spent decades—and I'm not alone in this—trying to convince people that animation isn't just commercial fluff—it's a powerful, multifaceted art form, often written off by both the general public and some artists who neither understand, care about, nor respect it.

When I started, there were few festivals. Animation schools were rare. Cartoon Network didn't exist. I began in the early 1990s as a festival entry coordinator, dealing with VHS tapes, ¾-inch reels, 16 mm and 35 mm prints—real, physical objects. Now everything arrives digitally. Not only that shift made things faster and more accessible, but it's also made the process feel less personal.

Independent films have changed, too. A generation ago, few addressed mental health, addiction, or trauma. Today, these subjects dominate. Sometimes, it feels like we've turned inwards so completely that we've lost sight of the world around us. If ever there was a time to look outward again, it's now.

Programs such as the CEE Workshops have professionalized independent animation, helping many artists. But that same structure can flatten the raw, personal expression that once defined indie work. I worry we're importing too much of a live-action, industry-driven mindset into a medium that thrives on individuality, experimentation, and a DIY mentality.

Yes, DIY can be lonely and difficult at times, but the results can be worth it if you carve your own path, and, frankly, when I look back at some of the most—at least for me—interesting voices, they were self-taught. They learned by trial and error, by absorbing any and every animated film they could find (and this was pre-YouTube days when that was no easy task). Today it feels like kids have been brainwashed into thinking they need animation schools or some specialized training. I don't mean to diss all education. There are some outstanding animation schools (e.g., the Rhode Island School of Design) that really exist to serve the students and help them find what is already within—and to get it out.

Unfortunately, too many schools are focused on training students for studio jobs and fail to give them a well-rounded artistic education. It's disappointing to encounter students whose knowledge of animation is limited to Pixar, Disney, Netflix, or Miyazaki. I'm a writer. I want to read everything, from as many diverse voices as I can. Same with music; I listen to almost any genre. Sadly, there are more and more students (more so in North America) who don't have a clue who Norman McLaren, Fyodor Khitruk, Run Wrake, etc., are. I blame this squarely on teachers and institutions established solely to train students for studio jobs.

-

The title of this book, *Watch Me Jumpstart*, comes—to the surprise of no one who knows me—from a Guided by Voices song. That phrase sums up how I've moved through this field—charging ahead without credentials, figuring it out as I went. Like when I took on a festival-organizer role I was wildly unqualified for.

IMAGE 0.1 Tom McSorley and Kelly Neall

-

Warning, while there is some chronological order, I often tend—as anyone who read my writing has likely encountered before—veer off the road at times. While I was writing this book I happened to be reading Fernando Pessoas' brilliant, annoying, and exhausting *The Book of Disquiet*. This "factless autobiography" is a non-linear work that contains introspective fragments to reflect the inner life of the protagonist.[1]

As I sit trying to recall the last 35 years, well, my memory works in a similar way. Things come to be in fragments and sometimes out of order. A memory from 1992 might instantly take me down a different path for a few paragraphs.

-

Before we get into the rest, I want to thank Tom McSorley, who gave me a shot that led to the OIAF and this life in animation. And Kelly Neall, my closest friend, colleague of 34 years, and co-parent of two sons (who both grew up with the OIAF and sometimes wished they had more "normal" parents, though I've got a feeling they'd change their minds fast once they saw how boring those people are). Without Kelly's vision, patience, and sacrifices, I would've run the festival into the ground years ago. Thank you both for everything.

And big thanks to Richard O'Connor, who's been a friend and colleague for about 30 years. He graciously took the time to read my first draft and offered sharp suggestions for improving my often fragmented and hurried approach.

Other huge thanks to Jarvis Neall, Harrison Neall, John Connolly, Tom Knott, Otto Alder, Linda Simensky, Ellen Besen, Marc Glassman, Marv Newland, Gerben Schermer, Michael Fukushima, David Verrall, David Ehrlich, Priit Pärn, Janno Põldma, Mati Kütt, Andreas Hykade, Theodore Ushev, Dan Sarto, Ron Diamond, Amid Amidi, John Libbey, the late Emru Townsend (*FPS Magazine*), Keltie Duncan, Devin Hartley, Maral Mohammadian, Azarin Sohrabkhani, Anastasiya Verlinska, Igor Prassel, Pilar Newton, Brent Smith, and the quartet of like-minded twits: Joni Männistö, Petrit Gora, Marko Tadić, Yiorgos Tsangaris.

Lastly, to all my past and present OIAF colleagues and the gang at Animateka (the mistress to my OIAF "wife" since around 2018). Thank you.

NOTE

1 Fernando Pessoa, *The Book of Disquiet*, translated by Richard Zenith (London: Penguin Classics, 2001), p. 12.

CHAPTER 1

Getting in Tune

My childhood was no more or less interesting than most, but the more I've thought about my years in animation, the more I see how that period heavily influenced my approach to programming, writing, onstage hosting/moderating, and sequencing films. I can honestly say I've never loved animation in the sense of obsessing over it. It never hit me the same way music, comedy, or even sports did. But then, in general, I've never been one to get overexcited about much—at least outwardly.

My earliest memory of anything to do with animation comes from around 1976 or 1977. I remember seeing *Pete's Dragon* at the Nelson Theatre in Ottawa. The most significant part of that memory wasn't the film, but the fact that the Nelson later became the ByTowne Cinema—the main venue since the early 2000s for the Ottawa International Animation Festival (OIAF).

Around that same time, I stumbled upon *Monty Python's Flying Circus*, which was playing on one of our television channels on Sunday evenings (I think). That I was allowed, at age nine or ten, to watch Python is pretty incredible. I'd first heard them—like most comedy—on Dr. Demento's radio show, which my parents played on weekends. I loved it. I couldn't wait to hear what bizarre thing was coming next. There were "Shaving Cream," "Hello Muddah," "It's a Gas" (the belching song), but also Peter Sellers, Abbott and Costello's "Who's on First," Python bits like "Spam" and "I'm a Lumberjack." And—I might be wrong here—I feel like I heard George Carlin's infamous "Seven Words You Can Never Say on Television." More likely, I heard it at an adult party my parents hosted or dragged me to. Either way, I remember being so pleasantly shocked by that routine.

DOI: 10.1201/9781003633181-2

Meanwhile, the Python series often went over my head. But unlike my adult years, back then I couldn't wait to see Terry Gilliam's insane collage animation shorts. They were silly, naughty, and ridiculed every aspect of society—especially the state, the church, and stuffed-shirt authority figures.

Although I hated it at the time, I am somewhat glad that my parents refused—for the most part, four of us lived on my stepfather's police salary—to splurge on cable. It pissed me off that I couldn't see the "cool" cartoons like *Super Friends!* Today, with a never-ending sensory assault, where everything is available, I look back more fondly and miss those days of only having access to three or four channels.

The only other animation I remember encountering regularly was *The Bugs Bunny/Road Runner Hour*, which aired on Saturday afternoons. I didn't know then that it was a compilation of vintage Looney Tunes and Merrie Melodies cartoons. I never much cared for the Road Runner or Tweety cartoons, but I loved anything with Bugs and Daffy. In hindsight, it makes sense. Their dynamic—along with that of Elmer Fudd, Yosemite Sam, and the rest—resembled the great comedy teams: the Marx Brothers (Bugs' persona was clearly inspired by Groucho Marx), Laurel and Hardy, and, in particular, Abbott and Costello.

So even from the get-go, the animation I enjoyed most skirted the borders of the comedy world. Fittingly, on those same Saturday afternoons, I'd often catch an *Abbott and Costello* movie. I loved their constant clashing and ingenious wordplay. It was outrageous stuff, and again, there was an anti-authoritarian vibe—let's just mess around with anyone and everyone.

While that was the extent of my animation roots, comedy was something I devoured. I loved everything Steve Martin put out and soon ventured into Richard Pryor, Robin Williams, and George Carlin. That passion for stand-up comedy has never left.

The other key comedy revelation came from television as well. It was a weekly sketch-comedy series featuring a bunch of unknown actors. SNL? Hell no. Sure, I enjoyed SNL, but it was a farm team compared to the genius of Canada's *SCTV*.

SCTV was a low-budget sketch-comedy series featuring Eugene Levy, John Candy, Joe Flaherty, Dave Thomas, Rick Moranis, Martin Short, Harold Ramis, Catherine O'Hara, and Andrea Martin. It was about as quirky and Canadian as you could get, yet with tinges of utterly obscure

IMAGE 1.1 Abbott and Costello

and bizarre Hollywood (*Taxi Driver* with Gregory Peck, Liberace's Christmas special with Orson Welles) and international references (e.g., Jerry Lewis doing Bergman's *Scenes from an Idiot's Marriage*, Bergman's *Winter Light* performed by a frat group in a phone booth) and just so many insanely inventive weirdo characters (Edith Prickly, Johnny LaRue, Dr. Tongue; most famous were the McKenzie Brothers, a clichéd, beer-swilling Canadian duo created largely to pad Canadian-content requirements for the broadcaster). *SCTV* was so wonderfully Canadian. It was like our secret, though not for long, as most of the cast went on to become stars in the U.S.

Comedians gave me permission to rebel, to question everything thrown at us that we were told was natural, proper, good, or normal. It was also an escape—and a defensive tool—while living in a rather cold and chaotic home that felt more like a boarding house than a family home. I felt alone for most of my childhood. Our family was not exactly close. There was no intimacy, no embraces. And then, as now, I was not good at socializing. I just didn't get it, so most often I stayed in my room where, by high school, I had my own phone line and a stereo system with many records and tape cassettes.

Most of my socializing came through sports. I played soccer, football, swimming, and baseball in local leagues. I was obsessed with all things hockey. I could never skate well enough to compete, but I played it anywhere possible—on ice, on the road, in parking lots, in parking garages. I collected hockey cards and even made up my own games with those cards and dice (I re-created hockey seasons long before EA Sports video games came around!).

By high school, music took over my life. I became obsessed with all manner of music. I suspect that, like comedy and sports, it was an escape from a social world I didn't understand or feel I fit into. Like many of my generation, I grew up around radio. I absorbed the latest songs from the constant Top-10 countdowns. Through the radio, I was exposed to all kinds of music, but it was in high school that I discovered the music that resonated most.

I entered high school in 1981 at age 13—perfect timing, musically. The older students had come out of the 1970s, so on our high-school radio show, I heard all kinds of vintage rock: Led Zeppelin, The Beatles, The Kinks, The Rolling Stones, Grateful Dead, and The Who. The Who would be the band that enraptured me most. Then there was my generation: we were coming of age alongside U2, R.E.M., The Cure, The Smiths, Midnight Oil, and others. It was a pretty amazing time to live between these two worlds—not to mention still catching late-1970s bands like The Jam, The Clash, and XTC. I suspect I learned more about music during my five years at Brookfield High School than in any of my actual classes (aside from literature).

When Grade 10 started in September 1982, there was a heavy buzz about The Who's so-called farewell tour (and in 2025, they embarked on their absolutely final tour), culminating in a final show in Toronto that December—televised for all to see.

I watched the concert with a friend in our basement and was immediately hooked. Strangely, my initial attraction was to bassist John Entwistle. He played loud and like a lead guitarist, but stood there stone-faced most of the time, à la Buster Keaton. I loved the contrast—it mirrored my own deadpan expression.

IMAGE 1.2 The Who

Soon, though, after hearing more albums, I was all about Pete Townshend—the way he used his guitar like a weapon, doing crazy windmills, blasting out angry power chords, jumping all over the place. There was a defiance and aggression that mirrored my own state of life, growing up in a home that wasn't particularly cozy and struggling daily to fit in without seeming like an oddball. (It would be more than 40 years later that I'd be told I have what was then called Asperger's syndrome, a mild form of autism.)

At the time, I had no idea. I just knew I struggled to fit in, wasn't the best team player, hated being stuck in classes, sitting at a desk for seven hours while passionless teachers droned on.

At 14, I bought my first guitar from my schoolmate, Alan. It was a heavy Epiphone. I had no idea how to play, so my mother signed me up for lessons. They were great at first. I just wanted to learn songs. The first ones I learned were "Hey Jude," "Yellow Submarine," and "Who Are You." Once we got into theory, I got bored and overwhelmed and quit.

From there—as I would later when I took over the OIAF and started writing and programming—I taught myself, sitting for hours in my bedroom, listening to a song on vinyl, trying to play along. In those days there were no guitar-tab websites, no internet. You either subscribed to *Guitar Player* magazine and hoped they'd feature something you liked in tablature, or you just figured it out yourself. I figured it out myself.

After playing with some friends, I joined bands (Ten Miles High, The Crowd Theory) and played shows in and around Ottawa before leaving that route behind in my early 20s.

During that time, I devoured music. Aside from the radio, there was Columbia House: ten records for a penny, then you had a year to buy a few more at regular price. They rarely offered what I wanted, so I often grabbed random albums. Soon, I had five or six milk crates of vinyl—all kinds of music.

Portability was an issue. If you wanted to walk around with a Sony Walkman or "ghetto blaster" (portable cassette player), you had to either buy music on cassette or record your vinyl onto blank cassettes. Cassettes were unreliable. Sure, vinyl could scratch or warp, but cassette tape regularly got stuck in the machine—sometimes salvageable with a pencil, often not. So most of us relied on vinyl and later CDs. (I remember being promised CDs were "much more durable." What nonsense. Younger generations would eventually re-embrace vinyl, which turned out to be more durable than cassettes, CDs, or whatever digital format came along.)

If you wanted to share music, you transferred songs from vinyl onto cassettes. The "mix tape" was an art form for my generation—compilations for lovers, friends, or yourself. You made mixes by theme, genre, artist, even instrument. And no mix tape was complete without a handmade cover, decorated with coloured markers or pencils.

After finally finishing high school in 1985, I applied to Carleton University in Ottawa. I had no clue what to study, so I did a sampler. After about two months, I dropped out. I returned the next fall and decided Political Science was the future. One of my electives, though, would prove far more enticing: Film History 101 (or something like that).

In what might have been the first class, we watched Alfred Hitchcock's *Rear Window*. It blew me away. I'd never thought about what happened off the screen—how films were made, the intent behind them. I'd only ever thought about content. This class ripped open my eyes. I saw how Hitchcock manipulated the audience while also commenting on cinema's voyeurism.

IMAGE 1.3 The Crowd Theory in 1988

After class, I switched my major to Film Studies.

For the next two years, I loved discovering cinema I'd never encountered—old, new, short, long, from every corner of the globe. Bergman, for whatever reason, appealed to me the strongest during those years (to the scorn of classmates who preferred Jean-Luc Godard).

And it wasn't just history; there was a strong theoretical aspect. Cultural Studies had hit the cinema world, and we examined films through the lenses of Michel Foucault, Roland Barthes, Jacques Lacan, and Pierre Bourdieu.

After two years, I decided I wanted to touch film—to make one. I applied to Sheridan College (home of Canada's oldest and most famous animation department), though I wasn't studying animation but Media Arts. For the application, we had to submit a visual art piece. I made a video featuring my grandparents and a balloon—probably with a Bergman *Persona* reference.

I got in.

It didn't go well.

There were maybe 25 of us that year; only five returned (four of those five, including me, ended up having long careers in the arts). It wasn't that the programme was terrible, but most of us wanted to make our own work, not train for industry jobs, which was the programme's focus. We had to take film, photography, audio, TV, and more. All we wanted was to experiment.

The one saving grace was Canadian filmmaker Phil Hoffman, whose work I would later write about. He encouraged personal experiments—creating from what you know and have experienced. Taking his words to heart, I made *The Man Who Would Be Fruit*, about a guy who turns into a tomato (yes, there was debate about whether a tomato is a fruit or vegetable), and *Pylon Man*, about a guy who believes a pylon cone on his arm grants instant superpowers.

In short: silly work, born of my comedy leanings.

That year, *Twin Peaks* first aired, and our class gathered every weekend to watch the latest episode. Meanwhile, we kept pushing our boundaries—nude pieces, showing up to audio class hammered (I later fell asleep on a train and woke up 60 km past my stop). My favourite stunt came in our TV class, where we had to make a sitcom pilot. I pitched a family of Elvis impersonators. Their doorbell played the opening riff of "Hound Dog," and a family member would enter into a spotlight, strike a hip pose, and say, "Thank you, thank you very much."

The teacher was not impressed. Minutes after we left class, the tape disappeared—our Elvis pilot gone. She denied it was intentional, but I have no doubt it was at least "accidentally on purpose."

That was probably the end of the rope for me at Sheridan. I stayed until the end of the semester but knew I wouldn't return.

I came back to Ottawa in late spring 1990, planning to finish my Film Studies degree. I took over a tiny downtown apartment from an ex-girlfriend. No kitchen—just a mini-fridge and two burners. Dishes in the bathtub.

To pay for this luxury, I got a job at a downtown parking lot. I sat in a booth all day, reading books and trying to invent a new English alphabet to eliminate redundancies. That crappy, low-paying job would somehow reward me decades later.

I quit at summer's end and joined Greenpeace as a door-to-door fundraiser. It didn't go well.

I disliked socializing, especially in that context. I don't know what I was thinking. I guess I thought it would look good on my résumé. I hated talking to strangers, and I didn't know squat about the environment or who was doing what to whom. And you only got paid when you got donations. It was just an awful experience and ended with a guy chasing me off his lawn. I worked there for maybe two weeks and didn't earn a dime.

In September 1991, I headed back to Film Studies at Carleton University. I then landed a part-time job as a class film projectionist. Back then, 16 mm prints were often screened during the classes and, since you didn't really need to be a union projectionist, I had just enough experience to get the job. It was great, too, because you also got to sit there and watch films from other classes.

Even though I was paying for university through a combination of grants and loans, the projectionist job wasn't enough to live off, even while living in a dump of an apartment.

During my first week or two back at Carleton, a classmate told me the Canadian Film Institute (CFI) was looking for a box-office manager—and that I should apply.

Within a week, I was walking into the offices of the CFI. It was located in the Arts Court, a century-old courthouse and jail that had been transformed into a cultural space for local arts groups. I arrived and was hastily introduced around: Brian, who looked after the non-theatrical division; Lynn, the accountant; John, the Executive Director; and finally Tom McSorley, the Programmer of the CFI cinema.

I have zero recollection of the actual interview, except that I believe I still had hints of orange dye in my hair (left over from my ill-advised hair-dye experiment just after leaving Sheridan College that spring) and was wearing a pinstriped jacket. The only question I remember—because Tom and I still joke about it—was when he asked if I was bilingual. My response was simply: "Well, I worked in the Market."

See, the ByWard Market was the city's tourist hub and the place we youngsters went to drink and socialize. It was the central spot of Ottawa life. As for bilingualism, I guess in my head I thought that working in this high-traffic area, not far from the Quebec border, somehow made it obvious I'd have knowledge of French. What I thought was a perfect example of clever equivocation actually makes zero sense to me now.

Well, it didn't matter. I got the job. Tom must have seen something he liked—or maybe the other candidates were really bad, assuming there even were other candidates. I never actually asked him. Maybe it's best I don't.

At the time, I was just relieved to have another job. I just needed the money, and having "Canadian Film Institute" on a résumé, especially for someone studying film, would look impressive for future job applications. Little did I know there would not really be any more applications. The CFI job turned into an opportunity that would completely change the course of my admittedly rudderless life.

CHAPTER 2

Summer Days

My unanticipated debut at the Canadian Film Institute (CFI) was on September 18, 1991. There was one film playing that evening: *Friends, Comrades* by Rauni Mollberg. That's about all I remember of that first night.

My job was pretty simple. I worked two or three nights a week. Everything was by hand. I had to collect the cash float, grab the box-office forms, and bike to the National Archives of Canada auditorium where the films were screened. (On Tuesday nights, we screened films at the then–Canadian Museum of Civilization in Gatineau, on the Quebec side of the Ottawa River. They already had their own staff, so it was on me to bike over there and sell CFI membership cards to anyone who might want one.)

The CFI regulars were an odd bunch, a gaggle of cinema-literate misfits. Some were shameless in the way they'd try to rip us off (reusing "free admission" cards they'd been given). Some were just utterly rude and entitled. Thankfully, on occasion a projectionist would have a big chunk of hash (that looked like a big chocolate bar) and we'd share a smoke. Soon, all the audience problems vanished.

Aside from doing box office and ushering, it was up to me to pay the projectionist at the end of each night (when we actually made enough money!). On non-screening days, I had to coordinate getting the film prints to and from distributors or other venues. Beyond that, I helped with distribution of our bi-monthly screening calendar. I'd package the calendars up and walk or bike them around town to assorted shops and restaurants. Eventually, I started helping write the calendars, roughing

DOI: 10.1201/9781003633181-3

IMAGE 2.1 Chris Robinson, CFI offices, 1994

out media releases, and occasionally even programming. My first programming attempt was a Woody Allen/Ingmar Bergman mini-festival. I lined up Allen films with the Bergman works that clearly inspired them. I was instantly hooked on programming.

So, just what was this CFI? Well, I'll tell you. It was founded in 1935 as the National Film Society (the name changed sometime in the 1950s). It was the first film society in Canada, and over the years the CFI played a pivotal role in the exhibition, distribution, and archiving of films. The CFI was the first film archive in Canada to be recognized internationally. The first post-secondary courses were rooted in the initiatives of Canadian film historian Peter Morris (who worked at the CFI). Canada's Oscars—the Canadian Screen Awards—have their roots in the CFI. Some of the first publications about films and filmmakers were published by the CFI, and the Toronto International Film Festival (TIFF) and Cinematheque Ontario owe some of their beginnings to the CFI.

Unfortunately, by the time I arrived, this thriving institute that had as many as 30–40 people working for it at one time was a shell of itself. As I mentioned in the previous chapter, there were just a handful of people there: Brian oversaw non-theatrical services. The CFI rented out assorted videotapes and 16-mm film prints to schools across Canada. They also received money to take care of a UNESCO collection. All of this was housed in the basement of the Arts Court building near our storage area in a handful of disused jail cells. Tom was the Director of Programming, overseeing the CFI's steady stream of film presentations. John Connolly was the Executive Director of the organization and worked on soliciting grants and doing year-end reports. Then there was Lynn, the accountant (I never understood why an organization this small required a full-time bookkeeper).

After a few months, I came into the office one day and met another staff member. His name was Tom Knott. He'd been away in Los Angeles, and it seemed he ran another division of the CFI: the Ottawa International Animation Festival (OIAF).

In early 1992, I officially started doing work for the OIAF. My initial job was to oversee the processing of each and every film submission that was mailed in. These films were candidates for the OIAF's short film competition.

Back in those days, animation festivals were still biennial because you didn't get a lot of turnover with new films. There were four main festivals: Annecy, France (the oldest and largest in the world), Animafest Zagreb (founded in 1972), the OIAF (founded in 1976), and Hiroshima (1985). These festivals all functioned under the approval of ASIFA (the International Animated Film Association). ASIFA, then as now, was a volunteer organization of animators from around the world. Animation festivals were originally founded to provide a space for non-commercial animators to showcase their films. It was also an important meeting point for artists from both the West and those living behind the so-called Iron Curtain.

ASIFA helped to establish an assortment of rules and regulations that strove to protect individual filmmakers. And back then the festivals were quite cooperative with each other. Everyone had their sort of set space. Annecy was held in June during odd years, Zagreb in June during even years, and Hiroshima and Ottawa were held during even years as well.

Now, of course, I later learned there were other animation festivals in Stuttgart, Utrecht, and Portugal (*Cinanima*), but they weren't under the umbrella of ASIFA for various reasons.

The OIAF had its ups and downs. After holding three festivals in Ottawa, the CFI was allegedly facing a sizable deficit and couldn't organize the festival anymore—oh, and for the record, the festival directors back then were Wayne Clarkson (1976), Frederick Manter (1978), and then Kelly O'Brien (1980, 1982). In 1984, the OIAF shifted to Hamilton, Ontario, where it had five festival directors including Tom Knott and Frederick Manter. Kelly O'Brien returned—as did Manter in a Producer role—when the festival then shifted to Toronto for its 1986 event. According to a few people who attended the festivals in those years, the Hamilton and Toronto events were unmitigated disasters. Finally, Frank Taylor, Executive Director of the CFI, brought the OIAF back to Ottawa under the CFI banner in 1988, where it has remained up until the time this book hit the presses.

I knew none of this in 1992.

Where were we? Right, my job. So, each day, I'd go down to the mailroom and gather up the piles of packages sent to us. Usually I had to bring a big bin or trolley to collect them all. Then, once back at the office, I'd open up every package. For each submission I'd grab a paper file folder that would end up holding the entry form, stills, biography, and whatever other printed materials were sent.

But before that I had to type the entire entry form into our computer database (I have no idea what programme it was!). It was pretty tedious work, but I enjoyed discovering all these new faces, places, and films. I swear I learned more about the world (postal codes, different spelling, Cyrillic, cities, countries) from this work than I ever got from a high school geography or history class. Hell, combined with my Film Studies courses, I learned about the world via cinema (not necessarily a good thing, as suggested in Priit Pärn and Janno Põldma's 1995 short animated masterwork, *1895*, but we will get to the Estonians later).

After typing in all the pertinent information, I'd then print off labels that had the title, director, category, and entry number. Then I'd stick one on the file folder and another on the VHS, ¾-inch tapes, or the film cans. The folder would be filed away in a metal cabinet (one of many we had), while the films would be placed on shelves or assorted bins. A lot of office space was occupied by these materials.

When I hear animators complain today about the festival process, I just shrug. They have no idea how easy it is today. Imagine, animators before the end of the 20th century had to manually submit to each festival. This meant not just having to write out each entry form but also having multiple stills printed, extra film, or video copies and then walking to the post office and paying to ship it all to a festival. I have a tough time sympathizing with contemporary animators who can easily cut and paste their info into a festival's online entry form, can digitally produce stills, and, easiest of all, just send us a link to their entry.

IMAGE 2.2 OIAF94 Staff & Selection Committee. Left to right – Otto Alder, Chris Robinson, Marc Glassman, Linda Simensky, Elaine Pain. Kneeling: Tom Knott

These were also the days before the internet. There was no social media to amplify marketing or calls for entries. In those days, we had to design and print the entry form each year along with accompanying newsletters—mailed out twice a year—that provided brief details about the upcoming festival.

The next step came in the summer. The OIAF, like all the ASIFA festivals back then, had an international selection committee chosen each year. Those four or five members would then be flown to Ottawa, put in hotels, fed during the week, and then required to go through each submission. For the tapes, we'd watch them in and around the office, but for the films, we'd have to book the National Archives cinema for a couple of days.

My next OIAF job was to oversee and coordinate the selection committee during their stay. That meant providing breakfast, taking them for lunch and dinner, etc., and then either playing the tapes for them or being the liaison between them and the film projectionist. Then as now, a submission was stopped when the committee unanimously agreed. Every so often, one stubborn committee member would insist on watching the rest of the film or having it fast-forwarded (as if expecting a miracle, one that almost never came). I recall a lot of exasperated committee members impatiently waiting for that last stubborn member to see the light and stop the entry that had no shot at getting in. One year I went through their notes (we gave them binders with printed sheets inside for each entry!) and one committee member had made a drawing of another being strung up on a rope. We'd sometimes make time to go through their notes, which ranged from thoughtful comments on a work to utter hatred of a film.

The cinema screenings were a bit trickier. There was no fast-forwarding. It was all or nothing. As always, committees started slow, getting a feel for the films and each other, but usually by day two they were starting to go through things faster... but yes, with film prints, it had to be unanimous to stop a film and you'd better be damn sure. Oh, and to make it exciting, there were occasional mishaps with the film prints. I recall one particular time when an inexperienced projectionist (we might have been forced to use him for whatever reason) arrived in bad shape, having just been dumped. Forlorn and unfocused, at least one film print caught fire because of his heartbreak.

Back in those days, they would vote through a scoring system that had been introduced at the OIAF by Prescott Wright in the 1970s. Completed sheets would be forwarded to Tom Knott in the office, and he'd input everything into the computer. Once they finished the films, they'd go through their shortlist and make their final decisions.

Once they were finished and out of town, the next step was notifying the filmmakers of the committee's decisions. Again, this involved designing, printing, and mailing. A pretty costly and tedious process compared to hitting a keyboard button today.

ASIFA-sanctioned animation festivals all had separate selection committees and juries (OIAF '92 used the same committee and jury because of budget problems). They would not only pay for the hotels and flights for the selection committee to come in the summer, but they also paid for them to return when the festival was on. This was on top of paying hotels and flights for the jury. It's insane when you think about all the money that went towards this (something that I'd remember when I took over the OIAF).

So, yeah, then that whole process of notifying the filmmakers, arranging the shipping of their screening copies—in those days, we paid to return all materials via ground shipping. We'd also sometimes have to work with other festivals to coordinate a film's arrival and departure. It was quite a nice collaborative initiative that festivals did back then; they'd gladly forward a film on to its next festival if the filmmaker asked.

Meanwhile, my other work involved mailing and distributing flyers, helping with the coordination of the programme books, and even driving to Montreal's Mirabel airport to collect guests. Back then, Montreal had two airports. Mirabel handled international flights, while Dorval (now called Montréal–Pierre Elliott Trudeau Airport) took care of continental ones. As such, it was easier to just send a driver to collect the international guests than have them transfer to Dorval. This was also another way I got to meet international animators and producers.

I still remember driving one animator back to Montreal after an OIAF. He was in bad shape. Not sure if he was hungover, but either way, he openly told me that he'd had an affair (yes, it happens a lot at festivals) and felt horrible about it since he was now returning to his wife and child. Being so naïve back then, I was shocked at what he was telling me and by the very notion that he was confiding in me, some nobody festival driver. I felt both shocked and appreciative that he felt like unloading such personal stuff onto me.

As I became a part of that community, I soon realized this was not an uncommon thing. A previous OIAF director met his wife during a festival. My three long-term relationships have all been with people working in animation (granted, Kelly was not in animation when we met). And while it's not always ideal (especially if that partner is a producer of short animation films that get submitted—festival programmers and producers are not a good mix), it's life. We're human.

The animation community is small and like a big family. The work often overlaps with your personal life. When you're travelling to festivals or organizing a festival, the people in that community are the ones you most often encounter and get to know. Film screenings aside, festivals are a communal experience with a lot of parties and social activities. And ask anyone who has travelled to festivals: it's a weird space where time slows. It reminds me of when I got high in Utrecht once. I was having a conversation with someone and I was sure it lasted for hours, but in reality it was about ten minutes. This is how the festival experience feels. It's like a month has been lived in that short time frame. And that's because you're living in full gear for five days. It's going first thing in the morning (depending on the depth of your hangover) and you're active, you're going to events, you're socializing constantly and going to dinners and parties. We're living in fifth gear at a festival. In 'regular' life, you're usually (at least I am) in first or second gear. It's an intense and exhausting experience. And yes,

OTTAWA 92 INTERNATIONAL ANIMATION FESTIVAL

FESTIVAL INTERNATIONAL D'ANIMATION OTTAWA 92

September 30 to October 4, 1992

30 septembre au 4 octobre 1992

GREETINGS

Preparations for the Ottawa 92 International Animation Festival are now in full swing. Once again the Festival will be held in Ottawa, Canada's capital, at the prestigious National Arts Centre, from September 30th to October 4th. We are confident that you will find our busy schedule of screenings, workshops and parties enjoyable and rewarding.

If you have any questions about Ottawa 92 please give us a call. We look forward to welcoming you to the Festival, to Ottawa and to our spectacular autumn colours.

SALUTATIONS

Comme vous le savez sans doute, l'édition 1992 du Festival international de l'animation d'Ottawa se tiendra du 30 septembre ou 4 octobre prochain, au prestigieux Centre national des Arts. Actuellement, nous mettons en oeuvre le maximum de moyens afin de régler les détails des programmes de films, des ateliers et des réceptions qui, nous l'espérons vivement, feront écho aux aspirations des professionnels et à l'enthousiasme du grand public canadien.

Nous comptons bien que vous partagerez avec nous cette célébration de l'art du cinéma d'animation, dans une ville fort accueillante, complètement ceinturée d'une nature abondante et éclatante de coloris automnal.

OFFICIAL COMPETITION

The awards jury/selection committee is comprised of: **Karen Aqua** (USA), director of NINE LIVES and KAKANIA; **Joyce Borenstein** (Canada), director of THE MAN WHO STOLE DREAMS and COLOURS OF MY FATHER; **Chris Casady** (USA), director of PENCIL DANCE, SHADRACH and principal of Roto Effects of America; **Mark Langer** (Canada), professor of Film Studies at Carleton University and author of many articles on the history of animation; and **Ellen Meske** (The Netherlands), director of THE INFLATABLE ALPHABET, the series "Schoon Genog" and numerous films for television.

COMPÉTITION OFFICIELLE

Le jury est composé de : **Karen Aqua**, réalisatrice de *Nine Lives* et de *Kakania* (É.-U.); **Joyce Borenstein**, réalisatrice de *Man Who Stole Dreams* et des *Couleurs de mon père* (Canada); **Chris Casady**, réalisateur de *Pencil Dance* et de *Shadrach*, et propriétaire de la Roto Effects of America (É.-U.); **Mark Langer**, professeur titulaire des Films Studies à l'université Carleton d'Ottawa et auteur de plusieurs ouvrages sur l'histoire de l'animation (Canada); **Ellen Meske**, réalisatrice d'*Inflatable Alphabet* ainsi que de la série *Schoon Genog* et de plusieurs téléfilms d'animation (Pays-Bas).

PROGRAMMES

A full slate of retrospectives and special programmes will be presented at Ottawa 92. These include:

KEN O'CONNOR: THE ART OF LAYOUT, a tribute to one of Disney's greatest artists, featuring excerpts from PINOCCHIO, FANTASIA, and DUMBO.

SHERIDAN COLLEGE: A SILVER ANNIVERSARY SALUTE to one of the world's leading schools of animation.

SHANGHAI ANIMATION STUDIO, a tribute to one of the world's most creative studios.

BRETISLAV POJAR, a retrospective look at Czechoslovakia's premier animation filmmaker.

RIGHTS FROM THE HEART, the premiere of this exciting new series from the French Animation Studio of the National Film Board of Canada.

HANS FISCHERKOESEN, a rediscovery of one Germany's pioneering animation filmmakers.

RECENT CUBAN ANIMATION, featuring films by Juan Padron, Tulio Raggi, Mario Rivas, Modesto Garcia, and Mario Garcia-Montes.

Several additional programmes and other Ottawa 92 surprises will be announced in the very near future.

PROGRAMMES

En plus de la compétition officielle, Ottawa 92 propose un tableau bien rempli de panoramas et de rétrospectives.

L'ART DU LAYOUT, SIGNÉ KEN O'CONNOR
Rétrospective de ce grand artiste de chez Disney, par le biais d'extraits de *Pinocchio*, de *Fantasia* et de *Dumbo*.

LE VINGT-CINQUIÈME DU COLLÈGE SHERIDAN Panorama de films réalisés par les étudiants de cette école d'animation d'excellente réputation internationale, qui fête son 25e anniversaire.

STUDIO D'ANIMATION DE SHANGHAI
Panorama de films produits par ce grand studio qui se trouve à la pointe de la création cinématographique en Chine et dans le monde.

BRETISLAV POJAR
Rétrospective saluant ce cinéaste comme un précurseur fort doué de l'animation tchèque et slovaque.

DROITS AU COEUR Première projection de cette nouvelle série de films palpitants, produite par le Studio d'animation française de l'ONF.

HANS FISCHERKOESON Rétrospective rendant hommage à cet ingénieux pionnier de l'animation allemande.

ANIMATION SI! Panorama de récents films d'animation cubains, mettant en vedette les cinéastes Juan Padron, Tulio Raggi, Mario Rivas, Modesto Garcia et Mario Garcia-Montes.

Les organisateurs annonceront bientôt la présentation de programmes supplémentaires et de films puisés dans la boîte à surprises du merveilleux monde de l'animation.

IMAGE 2.3 OIAF92 Newsletter cover

sometimes there is excess and questionable behaviour. It's also completely logical that you become closest with the people who are regularly sharing that similar intense experience.

Today, all of my closest friends are from animation. That was tough for me at first. My OIAF role gave me a name and some influence. Suddenly this eternally awkward person who never knew how to connect with people was more popular. People took interest in me. It was odd, and I certainly recall early on thinking that this felt disingenuous, that people were only feigning interest because they had this perception that I had power and influence as a programmer. I still feel this way, but I accept it. It's normal to some degree. If I left the animation world tomorrow, most of those friends and acquaintances would eventually fade from my life—not necessarily because I no longer have anything to offer them (in terms of selecting their films, let's say), but it's like when you leave high school or university or a job: you inevitably lose touch with those people and fall into new circles.

It's the same with each festival. Yes, we have some core staff, but there are a lot of temporary employees. For almost a year, you are involved with these people on a daily basis. You get relatively close by the time the festival rolls around. Organizing a festival is an intense experience that few animators or non-festival animation professionals have any appreciation for. Some people think it's just a five-day party that you can put together in your sleep. They have no concept of the amount of work that goes into preparing this so-called "five-day party." The endlessly long days and late nights. Work and personal life, at least for Kelly and me, overlapped all the time… which did not make for the healthiest of home environments. Kelly and I would be together as a couple for almost 20 years, and while working at the same job was not the primary cause of our splitting, it sure as hell didn't help. That said, we've now worked together another 15 years since we split and, for the most part, we're a solid team.

But I'm getting ahead of the story. I'll do that a lot. Some of this is chronological, but sometimes my memory will take us to other time periods. Maybe this structure is a bit like *Book of Disquiet*, itself consisting of many streams-of-consciousness fragments that maybe don't make sense in the moment but, when you reach the end, you can see how it all adds up.

I didn't do much at OIAF '92. I mostly sat at the media table in the National Arts Centre (then the sole space of the OIAF), once getting ripped into for the lack of French translation at the festival. In hindsight, the person was right, but they were also unnecessarily unpleasant and smug. And me being the contrarian, I'm sure I went right back at the guy. (Maybe this is why someone called me the John Woo of diplomacy once. Someone told me that I burst down the door and open fire before asking questions.) Other than briefly attending the opening party, I really didn't have much to do at the festival and went home most nights.

After it was all said and done, it was my job to help package and post back the films and any uncollected awards.

That first year with the OIAF was monumental for me. First, having to watch those 750 entries was mind-opening. I distinctly recall the thrill of seeing Raimund Krumme's *Crossroads*, Phil Mulloy's *Cowboys*, and *Ren & Stimpy* (where I learned that the creator was from Ottawa and attended the same high school as me). *Crossroads* and *Cowboys* had the most impact on me, largely because they were minimalist and looked like something anyone could do, yet within these deceptively simple and raw drawings were works that tackled themes of identity, masculinity, racism, etc.

At this moment I am looking back through the catalogue from that year, and the list of competition filmmakers is pretty close to an animation hall of fame: Caroline Leaf, Jerzy Kucia, Piotr Dumała, Stephen Hillenburg (pre-*SpongeBob*), Michaela Pavlátová, the strangely forgotten David Anderson, Joan Gratz, Georges Schwizgebel, Henry Selick, Barry Purves, Amy Kravitz, Wendy Tilby, Danny Antonucci, Paul Fierlinger, Gil Alkabetz, Co Hoedeman, and Igor Kovalyov.

What I most appreciated was that these artists were tackling some tough subjects, all within this short format. Over in Film Studies, I was being screened Bergman, Godard, Antonioni, Kubrick, Pasolini, and so much more, yet here were a bunch of "cartoons" tackling similar hefty ideas just as effectively, often under ten minutes.

From that moment, I never saw animation the same way.

Not long after, life returned to normal. I continued working for the box office/cinema department in between my film projectionist work and regular classes. Meanwhile, I'd started living with a young woman I'd been dating. Kelly Neall would not only play a pivotal role in my life, but she would soon have an enormous impact on the direction and success of the OIAF. I first encountered Kelly in 1991 when she worked at a vintage clothing shop. She had a unique, almost Louise Brooks–inspired look that caught my eye. Months passed and we met again at Carleton, where we were in the same film classes. When I finally got the nerve to ask her out, she gave me her number. A few days later, when I called it, it was a wrong number.

During the next couple of years, I added a new title to my CFI résumé: Director of Non-Theatrical Services. Brian had been let go from that position … and it was logical since we rarely rented out films anymore. I didn't care much for the job, but the title looked good on my résumé.

I can't even remember what I did. There weren't many film rentals anymore as the films and videos we had were becoming outdated and schools and libraries were switching to VHS and DVD. I do remember being assigned to go through every film and video in our collection and document it. This entailed spending many late nights in the allegedly haunted basement (I'm not the most present person, but I didn't get any ghostly vibes) of the Arts Court sorting through hours and hours of generally boring educational films.

I loved going through the films. It was just me in a small room using a Steenbeck editing machine to preview the content. The best part of that work was discovering these utterly cheesy old ephemeral films dealing with assorted things like smoking, drinking, driving, social mores, hemorrhoid removal, and highland sweater making.

For a brief period in the late 1990s, my friend and fellow troublemaker Lee Demarbre (now a respected cult filmmaker and co-owner of Ottawa's Mayfair Theatre) and I decided there might be an audience for these films. Working with local clubs, first Barrymore's and later Zaphod Beeblebrox, we started curating an evening called "Reel Mondays" (a really boring title, I might add). On the last Monday of each month, we'd host a silly screening of any outrageous works we could find in the CFI library.

Our pinnacle of infamy came during a Valentine's Day double bill when we showed the cult film *Nekromantik* alongside a documentary about pedophiles called *Chicken Hawk*. Yes, we were being little shit disturbers, but we had no idea it would unfold the way it did. Our press release for the evening landed at a local radio station just as the police chief was visiting. Someone passed it on to him, and suddenly, we were being investigated.

For the next 24 hours, we were one of the top news stories in town (competing with some wingnut who drove his car onto the Parliament Hill grounds). It was stressful but a fascinating look at how the media works and manipulates. If anyone had taken a moment—as the police did—to watch these "offensive" films, they'd have realized that the documentary was squarely critical of pedophiles and NAMBLA (the North American Man/Boy Love Association).

All this attention led to a phone call from someone I did not particularly want to hear from: my estranged stepfather, who was also an Ottawa police officer. He said he'd heard about what was going on, and I assured him there was nothing offensive (in fact, the fictional *Nekromantik* would likely gross out more people, but no one said a word about it). When showtime came,

OTTAWA 94
INTERNATIONAL
ANIMATION
FESTIVAL
SEPTEMBER 28 TO
OCTOBER 2nd, 1994

FESTIVAL
INTERNATIONAL
D'ANIMATION
OTTAWA 94
DU 28 SEPTEMBRE
AU 2 OCTOBRE 1994

Greetings Preparations for the Ottawa 94 International Animation Festival are now in full swing. The 10th edition of the International Animation Festival, taking place from September 28th to October 2nd at Canada's prestigious National Arts Centre, promises to deliver all the events that the Festival has become known for — the competition, retrospectives, tributes, workshops, Chez-Ani and the animators's picnic. We are confident that you will find our busy schedule of screenings, workshops and parties enjoyable and rewarding.

If you have any questions please give us a call. We look forward to welcoming you to the Festival, to Ottawa and to our spectacular autumn colours.

Official Competition From July 25th to August 3rd, the Selection Committee met to select the films and videos that will make up the Official Competition. We received over 800 entries from 40 countries. The Selection Committee consisted of: Otto Alder (Germany), Marc Glassman (Canada), Elaine Pain (Canada) and Linda Simensky (USA). The Jury members will be announced shortly.

Programmes A full slate of retrospectives and special programmes will be presented at Ottawa 94. Tributes confirmed at press time include: Vancouver animator Al Sens (A HARD DAY AT THE OFFICE); the director of HEAVY METAL Gerald Potterton; former UPA designer and director of THE CRITIC and FLEBUS, Ernest Pintoff; animation pioneer John Bray; and Croatian animator/director Borivoj (Bordo) Dovnikovic. Confirmed special programmes include: Hollywood Cartoons Produced in Cinemascope, programmed by noted animation historian Jerry Beck; Independent Animation from Australia; and Animated Women, documentary portraits of Faith Hubley, Joanna Preistly, Ruth Peyser and Lynn Smith. Additional details and programmes will be announced in August.

Bonjour Les préparatifs du Festival international d'animation d'Ottawa vont bon train. Cette 10e édition du Festival aura lieu au prestigieux Centre national des Arts, et ce du 28 septembre au 2 octobre 1994. Elle regroupera tous les événements qui font la renommée du Festival - compétition, rétrospectives, hommages, ateliers, Chez Ani et le pique-nique des animateurs. Nous sommes d'avis que vous trouverez notre vaste choix de films, d'ateliers et de réceptions particulièrement agréable et enrichissant.

Si vous avez besoin de renseignements supplémentaires, n'hésitez pas à entrer en contact avec nous. Nous nous faisons une joie de vous accueillir au Festival dans les splendides couleurs d'Ottawa en automne.

Compétition officielle Du 25 juillet au 3 août, le Comité de sélection se rencontrera pour choisir les films et vidéos qui entreront dans la catégorie de la Compétition officielle. Nous attendons plus de 800 films en provenance de 40 pays. Le Comité de sélection est formé de Otto Alder (Allemagne), Marc Glassman (Canada), Elaine Pain (Canada) et Linda Simensky (Etats-Unis). Les noms des membres du Jury seront annoncés sous peu.

Programmes Une grande variété de programmes spéciaux et de rétrospectives sera présentée à Ottawa 94. Les hommages aux personnes suivantes étaient confirmés au moment de l'impression: l'animateur de Vancouver Al Sens (A HARD DAY AT THE OFFICE); le réalisateur de HEAVY METAL, Gerald Potterton; Ernest Pintoff, antérieurement concepteur à la UPA et réalisateur de films tels que THE CRITIC et FLEBUS; John Bray, pionnier en animation; et Borivoj (Bordo) Dovnikovic animateur et réalisateur croate. Les programmes spéciaux incluront: Animation hollywoodienne produite en Cinemascope, programme annoté par Jerry Beck, historien en animation; Animation indépendante en Australie; et Femmes animées, portraits documentaires de Faith Hubley, Joanna Preistly, Ruth Peyser et Lynn Smith. La suite des programmes sera annoncée au mois d'août.

IMAGE 2.4 OIAF94 Newsletter cover

there were a couple of undercover officers in attendance (they were so obvious) and a few protesters out front. We were disappointed, though. We were sure we'd have a full house, but it wasn't quite the sellout we'd anticipated. After a few drinks, we chatted with the officers, who said they were actually just there to keep an eye on some known sex offenders.

While we did Reel Mondays for a couple of years and even got some decent local press and the cover page of our weekly arts paper, the Valentine's double bill was our peak performance. It was always a lot of fun (we also did trivia and gave out odd prizes we got at the erotic shop next door), and I do remember that we'd do pre-OIAF events for locals to get publicity for the festival. We'd find animation oddities like Todd Haynes's banned *Superstar*, animated porn, ephemeral animation shorts, and occasionally even some of the weirder entries we'd received at the OIAF.

Eventually, the non-theatrical services position ended when we were instructed to transfer all the films to the basement of the Cinéma Impérial in Montreal. So one night in the late 1990s, Lee and I and some others rented a truck, loaded it with piles of 16-mm prints (definitely in the hundreds), and drove through crappy snowy weather for over two hours to unload those prints in the basement. That was the last I ever saw of those prints. I suspect they're still gathering dust there today.

"Why the Cinéma Impérial?" you ask? Now, that is a valid question. So let's go back a bit.

In 1988, the struggling CFI was taken over—along with its debts—by Serge Losique, the infamous director of the World Film Festival in Montreal (which in those days was a far more interesting festival than TIFF in Toronto). Losique had created this thing called Cinémathèque Canada. Under that umbrella existed two divisions: the CFI and the Conservatoire d'art cinématographique (which was essentially an art-house cinema running out of Montreal's Concordia University, where Losique was teaching).

He was not an easy man to work with, but fortunately I rarely had to. If he was our Mr. Burns, I was Homer Simpson, in the sense that he had no idea who I was and forgot me the moment he left the office after one of his surprise visits to Ottawa. I sort of liked it that way!

While he has to be given credit for keeping the CFI alive, he enforced some questionable budget decisions that hurt the OIAF, turning it into a bare-bones operation in 1992 and 1994. I could say more, but there's no reason to repeat hearsay.

By the time OIAF '94 was rolling around, Kelly and I were living together and also working as teaching assistants in Film Studies at Carleton University. We loved that job and did it for a couple of years.

To this day, the Film Studies programme at Carleton and the CFI/OIAF have strong connections. I have no doubt that, statistically, we've been the leading employer of Film Studies graduates. Many of our key staff

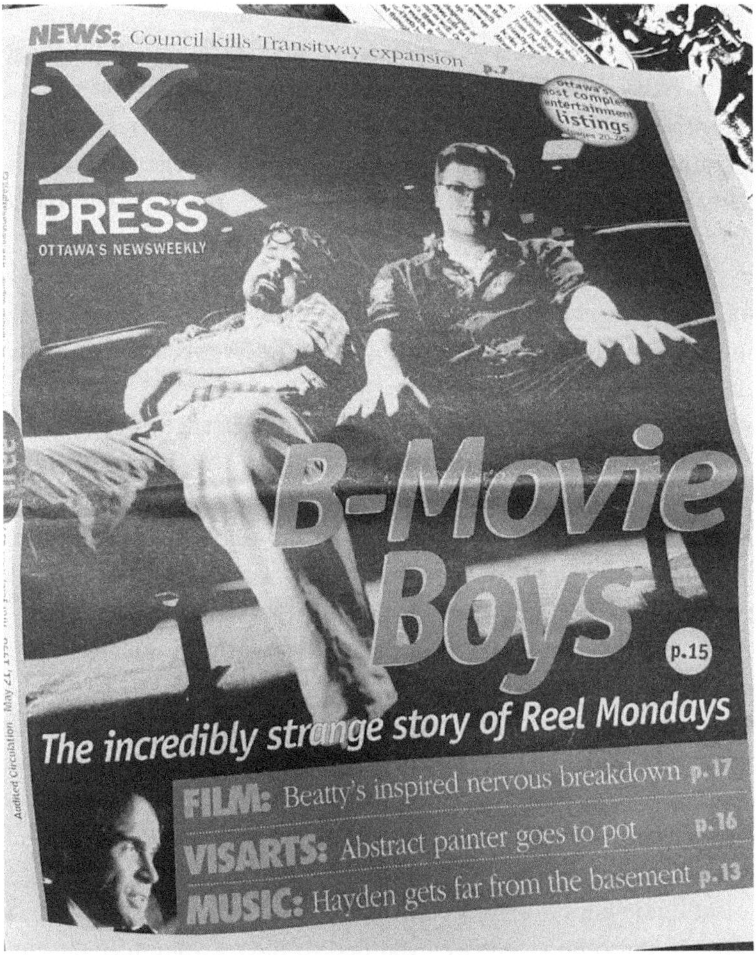

IMAGE 2.5 Chris Robinson and Lee Demarbre (Reel Mondays) on the cover of The Ottawa Xpress weekly paper

members came from the department, and even today Carleton graduate students can do an internship with either the CFI or the OIAF.

During this time, Kelly also had a job as an administrative assistant in the department, which was fantastic because we had access to their vast VHS collection. I guess we can admit this now that enough time has passed … but most nights she'd bring a film home and I'd dub it onto another VHS. Yes, kids, we didn't have cut-and-paste or uploading functions—just two VHS machines and blank VHS tapes. And there was no speeding up the process. You had to play the entire film while duplicating.

Okay, again, this doesn't necessarily have anything to do with my animation career, but it's a moment of nostalgia and context for those too young to have experienced these days before technological saturation. I almost miss those days—not because of the tedious process of making poor-quality bootleg VHS tapes, but because of the excitement we felt discovering rare works you couldn't find anywhere. Yes, it's great that today you can almost find everything, but it's also taken something magical away. Same with books and music. We used to spend hours browsing through bookstores and record shops, hoping to find something special … but today I can find anything in a few minutes on this very computer I'm typing these words on.

I don't remember a lot about the OIAF '94 preparations other than there being a bit of tension between Kelly and me and Tom Knott. There might have been a sense that we were doing more work than we should have been (to be fair, that happens every year—it's the nature of festival management). But by the time the OIAF '94 programme book went to print, the three of us were listed as co-directors. I couldn't recall what led to that, but Kelly did: "I remember Tom wanted us listed like that, but we didn't want to be listed as co-directors because we were afraid it would tank!"[1]

I was doing the same jobs as in 1992 but was also involved in overseeing the programme book design and the designer (who was our roommate that year). I continued to do airport driving and, during the festival, I was also assigned the task of being the stage manager. This meant sitting in the NAC theatre's projection booth and directing each screening. That meant overseeing some impatient union guys who took care of projection, sound, lighting, etc.

It was so old school that we even had to have a volunteer on hand to place a sock (yes, you read that correctly) over the video screen lens to block out the light when we were screening film. Turning the machine on and off meant waiting for the projector to reboot, and we had no time for that during a screening. Someone else was on the headset to coordinate where the filmmakers were sitting since each of them would be introduced after their film screened.

It was mostly a pretty fun job, though a few times the projections went wrong (usually with video), and I can remember some angry animators looking up toward the booth before racing up to bang on the door. That was a big mistake. Union projectionists took their job seriously but would not stand for dealing with any angry filmmakers. Mistakes happen. Live with it.

What I remember most about that position—aside from JJ Sedelmaier angrily glaring up at the booth after his short screening was muddled—was having a massive hangover one day after overdrinking on red wine with a selection committee member I'd gotten to know that year. I was so hungover that I remained drunk most of the day. Over the next few years, there would, unfortunately, be many more days like that.

In the meantime, Kelly had been hired on as a sponsorship assistant. She recalls: "The producer freaked out at the workload and quit, and then I got thrown in—young and with very little experience."[2] In those days, that basically meant overseeing every aspect of the festival: screenings, picnic, parties, volunteers, staff, everything. In other words, she was already doing the job she's now done as Managing Director for 26 years.

By this time, I was getting to know animation people a bit more. The selection committee that summer included Linda Simensky (then of Nickelodeon) and Otto Alder, a German-based programmer (formerly of the Stuttgart festival). There was also Marc Glassman, a film writer, programmer, and owner of Pages bookstore, the coolest indie bookstore in Toronto, and maybe Canada. I got to know all three quite well (especially Otto, who remains a good friend), and all three were very influential when I eventually took over as Executive Director of the OIAF.

Speaking of which, it was during OIAF '94 that we learned that Tom Knott was likely leaving the OIAF to become a recruitment director at Warner Bros in Los Angeles. The moment I heard these rumours, I pretty arrogantly decided that I could replace Tom, and I started actively talking to different people in the animation community (why? I have no idea—I guess I stupidly thought that outsiders would have some influence on OIAF decisions).

But I made no bones about it: I wanted the job. I was ambitious to a degree, but I think mostly I craved job security of some sort, and I thought (ha ha ha) running a major animation festival would be pretty close to having that.

Indeed, Tom Knott did leave after OIAF '94. Kelly also moved on. She had taken a full-time job with the Ottawa-Hull Film and Television Association (essentially the film liaison office of Ottawa).

Meantime, the CFI was not in good shape. By 1995, there was just Tom and me left in this big office space. And things were not looking good financially. When Serge Losique told us that he'd scored an extra $50,000 from a government funder, we felt great relief—until he then appointed his

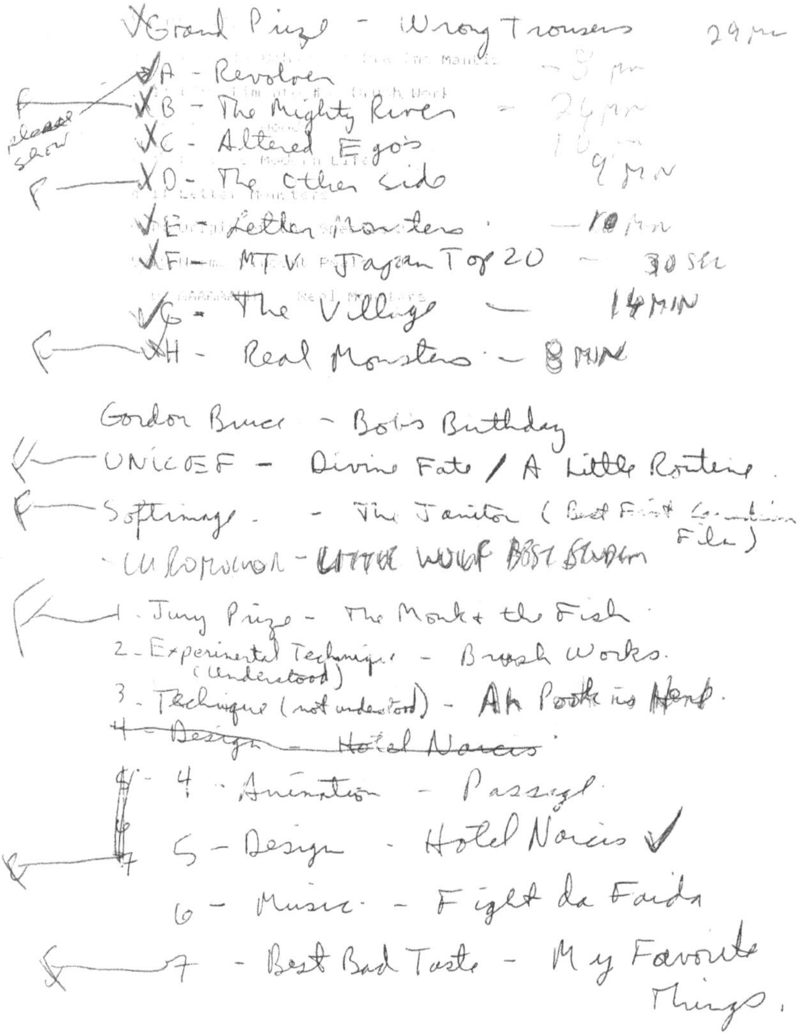
Grand Prize - Wrong Trousers 29 min
A - Revolver - 8 min
B - The Mighty River - 24 min
please show
C - Altered Ego's 10 min
D - The Other Side 9 min
E - Letter Monsters - 10 min
F - MTV Japan Top 20 - 30 sec
G - The Village - 14 MIN
H - Real Monsters - 8 MIN
Gordon Bruce - Bob's Birthday
UNICEF - Divine Fate / A Little Routine.
Softimage - The Janitor (Best First Commission Film)
Chromacolor - LITTLE WOLF BEST STUDENT
1. Jury Prize - The Monk + the Fish
2. Experimental Technique (understood) - Brush Works.
3. Technique (not understood) - Ah Pook is Here.
~~4 - Design - Hotel Narcis~~
4. Animation - Passage.
5 - Design - Hotel Narcis ✓
6 - Music - Fight da Faida
7 - Best Bad Taste - My Favorite Things.

IMAGE 2.6 Handwritten Jury notes – OIAF94

son, François, as the new director of the CFI. This was an utterly baffling move, as François had zero experience overseeing anything and there were only two of us to manage. It got worse. Tom and I, to this day, remember the sound of a truck backing up into the Arts Court loading dock. Inside were about $3,000 worth of bookshelves that François had ordered for the office. We laugh now, but at the time we were enraged.

So much for that $50,000.

It was a tense period. I got along pretty well with François, to the point where he once took me to lunch and offered me Tom's job as the programming director of the CFI. It was a job I'd have loved to have, but not like this. Even though Tom and I didn't always see eye to eye, there was no chance I was going to betray the very guy who gave me my start. I felt so uncomfortable during that lunch and immediately called Tom to tell him. I did, though, plant seeds with François that I'd be interested in taking over the OIAF. I explained that I'd worked on two festivals already and knew most of the ins and outs of the festival.

In early 1995, I was officially named Executive Director of the OIAF. I was paid a glorious $26,000 (Canadian) to be full time. And in those days, that was it—there were no other staff members until five to six months prior to the festival.

I've long made jokes about how I lucked out getting that job because of François not knowing any better. For a long time, I thought it was ridiculous that they hired me for this important position, but years later I learned that François had done some homework and consulted other people, including our fundraising director, John. John assured François that I could handle it and would thrive.

I would do okay eventually, but only after almost bankrupting the place.

NOTES

1 Interview with Kelly Neall, November 2025.

2 Interview with Kelly Neall, November 2025.

CHAPTER 3

Strutting, Skulking, and Stumbling (1995–2000)

1995. I am suddenly the youngest animation festival director around. I'm like a kid who just got his license but still lacks the basic experience and the unspoken or untaught rules of the road. And like those arrogant youth, I jump in the car and put the gas pedal to the floor. Sometimes the ride was smooth, sometimes it was downright terrifying.

One of the first things I did as the new director—after giving up my roles as the CFI's Assistant Programmer and Director of Non-Theatrical Services—was to cobble together an advisory committee. I knew I was potentially in over my head and would need some guidance. Thankfully I had access to some great and generous people: Mark Langer (OIAF '92 selection committee member and my old Film Studies professor); Linda Simensky, Otto Alder, Marc Glassman, Ellen Besen, and later Michael Fukushima (producer, National Film Board of Canada); Marv Newland, Gerben Schermer (more on him later), Jayne Pilling, and Maureen Furniss.

I've never been a person who likes—for better or worse—being told what to do, but in this rare case, I knew I was in over my head and needed guidance. Their insights were invaluable.

Meantime, two surprises greeted me in my new OIAF role.

First, Serge Losique insisted that we make the festival annual. Now, this was not necessarily a bad idea. With the animation industry expanding rapidly into commercials, television, and feature films—along with

DOI: 10.1201/9781003633181-4

the slow emergence of more schools, the internet, and technological advancements that were making the creative process a bit quicker—it made sense for animation festivals to switch from their traditional biennial status to annual. It turned out Annecy was doing it too. Still, this was my first damn year as the director—could I just focus on one festival for now!? Eventually I convinced Losique that we should do a smaller event during the off-season that focused solely on student films. The OIAF always had a student category and welcomed a lot of North American students, but we never really had enough space to show more student work. A student-focused festival would put them front and centre and would show many more student works, and students back then were in heavy recruitment mode, so I figured we'd capitalize. In the end I got the approval (or maybe I just did it without!) to introduce the Ottawa International Student Animation Festival (SAFO). SAFO would run for four editions before we finally decided in 2003 that it was time for the OIAF to be annual.

With SAFO, the OIAF became one of the first annual animation festivals (Annecy would follow a year later).

Secondly, I received an afternoon phone call from the then-named Ontario Film and Development Corporation (OFDC) telling me that they had cut about $100,000 from our funding for reasons that I honestly cannot recall at the moment. It might very well have been related to us not doing enough industry-wise (a valid critique of the bare-bones OIAF '92 and '94 editions). The irony, though, was that the industry was starting to explode at that time, and we were damn lucky to have the industry step in to replace that lost government money. In future years, there would be times when an increase in government funding helped make up for a lack of industry sponsorship during slow periods.

On a more positive note, in June 1995 I embarked on my first trip abroad, attending the Annecy Animation Festival in France. It was my first time on a plane (I remember being scared shitless by all the unfamiliar sounds I heard as the plane took off—for a few years I was a nervous wreck on planes; it's better now … it's airports and their Kafkaesque systems that wring my sanity today) and my first time representing the OIAF.

It's funny to look back and see how geeky I was. I bought a linen jacket, printed off OIAF final reports to present to the ASIFA-International Board. I was so naive I treated the ASIFA Board like it was our board of directors, only later realizing that was nowhere near the case and that I'd eventually start to turn my back on this well-intentioned but slightly feckless association of

IMAGE 3.1 Gerben Schermer, Tom Knott, and Chris Robinson at OIAF96

volunteers. I also had no idea how to travel. I hadn't planned for connections or for needing an extra hotel night. I'm still grateful to the late Michèle Pauzé from the National Film Board of Canada, who kindly shepherded me through Lyon train stations and airport hotels. She clearly saw how green I was.

That first festival was probably the only time I really prioritized screenings and networking. I went to four or five screenings a day. I hit a couple of parties, but I was tame compared to later, more alcohol-soaked festival trips. I was focused on representing the OIAF and meeting people. Linda Simensky, whom I'd met in 1994, helped a ton and introduced me to people, including Maureen Furniss.

Strangely (given that I was sober), I don't remember much else about Annecy except a heated argument with staff about getting into the awards ceremony—a ceremony that became a bit legendary for its chaos. Filmmakers were walking down to accept the wrong awards, that kind of thing. I'd heard stories about Ottawa '90 with the drunk Russians and mangled French, but this Annecy show was something else. I remember thinking: I never want Ottawa to become like this.

Even then, Annecy felt inaccessible. People spent their time in lines or trying to get into parties—parties that often weren't worth it. In Ottawa we've always tried to make everything accessible: screenings, parties, social stuff.

IMAGE 3.2 Gerben Schermer and Hotel kitchen staff, Stuttgart, 1996

I eventually stopped going to Annecy regularly and leaned into smaller, more intimate festivals that showed films I wasn't seeing elsewhere.

That said, we need Annecy. Like Toronto in Canada, people love to hate it because it's big and successful—and a bit showy—but everybody goes there. I just know I don't want Ottawa to become that big or that glossy. Annecy can stay #1; we're happy being the scruffier second.

Back home, I knew I needed a festival producer—someone to run events and manage staff. Kelly was the obvious choice, but she'd taken another job. So for a few years the position was tricky—not because the two people who did it from 1996 to 1999 were bad, but because they had to work with me: someone who was a mental/emotional mess at managing staff, budgets, and people. They ended up doing more than they should have because I disappeared into programming. I loved dreaming up programmes, and this was also the start of me really enjoying the writing side. What I didn't love was everything else: budgeting, proposals, parties, the Animator's Picnic, studio meetings, day-to-day staff stuff. In other words, the job.

In 1996, I travelled to more festivals—Stuttgart, Cardiff, Zagreb—meeting new friends and learning more about how festivals actually work. I met Peter Dougherty, Gerben Schermer, Jayne Pilling, Phil Mulloy, Kōji Yamamura … people who'd become lifelong friends and collaborators. Schermer especially—I'd count him as a brother and probably the biggest

IMAGE 3.3 Otto Alder and Chris Robinson, Animafest Zagreb, 1996

influence on me as a programmer/curator. We also liked to drink. A lot. Our first meeting in Stuttgart ended with me locked in my hotel room the next day with a brutal hangover.

What I loved was discovering festivals that were smaller than Annecy and felt more inclusive. Cardiff was where I met the late Peter Dougherty and first saw Run Wrake's work. Stuttgart was where I met Gerben, Mulloy, Andreas Hykade, and Priit Pärn. I felt way more at ease than I had at Annecy.

Zagreb, though, scared the hell out of me. This was near the end of the Yugoslav wars. Our hotel was surrounded by armed soldiers, and on every floor there were plainclothes guys in black with little mysterious bags. On top of that, the competition screenings were REALLY long—three hours with an intermission, plus a long, formal opening. For me it was unbearably dull. The best part was sneaking off to some castle ruins with Maureen Furniss and Norwegian animator/ASIFA guy Gunnar Strøm. The guard didn't mind us wandering around with a bottle of slivovitz.

During this time, something called the World Wide Web appeared. We'd started a website with the help of two local civil servants who did this on the side. Around then I met Ron Diamond from Acme Filmworks. He pitched me on this thing he called the Animation World Network (AWN)—a website that would gather parts of the global animation

IMAGE 3.4 Igor Kovalyov, Priit Parn, and Paul Driessen at OIAF96

community and even host festival sites. I was sceptical but figured, why not—let's try it. That started a relationship that's still going and that really opened the door for me as an animation writer.

We kept using a selection committee, because I didn't yet have the confidence—or the time—to handle submissions alone. I did, however, unofficially sit in as a fourth member (which probably annoyed them). Watching films get selected that I'd never have picked was frustrating. To make it less stiff, I gave each member a *Beavis and Butt-Head* remote with buttons like "Heh heh," "This sucks, change it," "That's cool," and "Don't make me kick your ass." Childish, yeah—but I've never liked the po-faced vibe of committees and juries.

Around the same time, I was getting annoyed with ASIFA. I didn't love being told which guests to invite or having to comp board members and give member discounts. I took it way too seriously back then, but it did lead to something useful. Ron's AWN had a monthly online magazine, *Animation World Magazine*, and they invited me to write about ASIFA. That turned into a pretty hostile multi-part exchange between me and various board members. I wrote things like:

> Yet some 37 years later in a drastically altered world, ASIFA-International appears to have lost its way. This once active and energetic association has become a bureaucratic 'old

> boy's club,' seemingly more concerned with the prestige and benefits of their position than with actively promoting 'the art of animation.' ... The ASIFA children's rights workshop ... reeks of a stifling political correctness.[1]

Later I took shots at ASIFA–Canada:

> The problems with ASIFA–Canada extend well beyond the festival. What appears to be a national association is, in reality, a Montreal-dominated chapter that's far too closely linked with the National Film Board of Canada to actually reflect and promote the many independent animators scattered across the country. (The recent creation of ASIFA–Vancouver was, in part, a response to this.) There are independent animators in Canada who don't work for the NFB and, if the ASIFA mandate means anything, their concerns should take priority over those of a government-funded—if shrinking—studio.[2]

Looking back, I wasn't wrong, but I was unnecessarily harsh and arrogant.

The end result was that the OIAF became the first of the ASIFA festivals to leave and say, thanks but no thanks.

As I mentioned, our government shortfall was offset by a rise in industry support. The timing couldn't have been better. With the introduction of animation-oriented places like Nickelodeon, Cartoon Network, Klasky Csupo, DreamWorks, along with Pixar, Disney, and Warner Bros., there was a gold rush of industry activity, and festivals like Annecy and Ottawa were beneficiaries because networks wanted animation, studios needed content and talent. More countries were taking advantage of this need and created animation-focused schools/departments.

I just remember there being an insane level of recruiting in those days. And also, what was cool was that studios back then looked at the short competition films to get new talents. *The Ren & Stimpy Show*, *Beavis and Butt-Head*, *South Park*, and, later on, *SpongeBob SquarePants*—all these talents were found at festivals or at unique animation screening events like *Spike & Mike's Sick and Twisted*. Looking back it was a pretty cool time. Festival animator Igor Kovalyov was recruited by Klasky Csupo after his controversial OIAF '90 Grand Prize winner, Hen, His Wife, was seen at Ottawa. Even hardcore indies like Piotr Dumala, The Brothers Quay, Jan Svankmajer, Jerzy Kucia, and Alexander Petrov got commercial work via festivals, as did many others, thanks to forward-thinking studio folks (MTV often commissioned indie animators for assorted spots/IDs).

It was really a pretty marvelous time, when studios were taking risks and actively looking for cool projects and artists. Today, you just don't see that anymore. They want talent that will fit seamlessly into their systems. They just don't take risks like they did, and the overall sameness—at least visually—of animation shows is ample evidence. I mean, just go look at the 1990s hits like *Rugrats* or *Aaahh!!! Real Monsters* and you will see East European animation influences all over them.

Oh, and on top of everything else going on during this first year, OIAF '96 also happened to be our 20th anniversary. To mark the occasion we invited all the past OIAF directors to attend the festival and say a few words in the programme book and at the opening. So: first time I'm directing a festival, and every previous director is in the house. No pressure.

Back then the festival home was Canada's prestigious National Arts Centre (NAC), a government-funded place for theatre, opera, music, etc. As a space, I didn't mind it: everything was in one building, which made things way easier to manage. But it was expensive, and we had to deal with a union that could make even the most pro-union person roll their eyes. You couldn't turn off a light or move a chair without a union person. We had to use their box office staff and a squad of uniformed ushers. From the start, the vibe felt wrong—too formal, too detached from our personality. Worse, the NAC staff we were paying for often didn't know anything about the festival or its schedule. They didn't care; we felt like an annoyance. For the awards show we were told that any costumes or performance-y elements meant extra charges. We weren't even allowed to place the awards on the table ourselves. That had to be a union guy. It was absurd.

It was a beautiful venue, but it didn't fit our evolving identity. I wanted something looser, more "street," spread across a few venues so people could actually see Ottawa. It wouldn't be long before we made big venue changes.

Even though I hadn't taken over competition selection yet, being in charge meant I did take over competition sequencing (I'll get into that later) and special screening selection.

Competitions celebrate current work; retrospectives and special programmes give people a sense of where the medium came from. Even now, with everything allegedly online, older animation isn't that easy to find unless you know exactly what you're looking for. And because there still isn't a ton of accessible, non-academic writing on global animation, these programmes are still necessary.

Special screenings can focus on a filmmaker, a studio, a technique, a country, or a theme. In North America—where, in my opinion, too many students know only Disney/Pixar/Ghibli/YouTube—festivals plug a real gap.

What drives me nuts is how many schools prioritize training for studios over nurturing artistic expression and then barely teach animation history. Lots of universities have Film Studies (with limited career prospects, as I learned), but almost nobody has Animation Studies. Everyone says, "Animation isn't a genre," and then schools treat it like one—just another class next to melodrama and horror. You expect that from the public, not from academia. And you can see it in the student films that are obviously made to please a recruiter who also doesn't know who Norman McLaren or Priit Pärn is.

And no, that's not "old man" talk. I felt this way in my late 20s.

Back to 1996. My own animation history knowledge was limited. I mostly knew the filmmakers who'd sent work to Ottawa. So the first retrospective I chose was Raimund Krumme. Krumme's poetic minimalism, the Beckett/Tolstoy echoes, and the "anyone could draw this" look really spoke to me. The other programme I put together was animation about hockey—because, well, Canadian.

Around this time I started getting published. Emru Townsend's *FPS Magazine* in Montreal mostly covered industry stuff, but I convinced him to let me write about Krumme and about hockey in animation. The pieces were stiff and way too academic, but Emru gave me a shot, and I'm still grateful. I even briefly edited the magazine, but my taste didn't match a readership that wanted tech and industry news, not some guy psychoanalyzing Estonians.

A big turning point came at Stuttgart in 1996, where I saw Pärn and Põldma's *1895*. It was everything I loved—funny, dense, film-literate, and critical of cinema's power to shape and misshape how we see the world. Otto Alder introduced me to them afterwards; we drank and talked, and that led to our big Estonian retrospective at OIAF98, trips to Tallinn, and eventually my book *Between Genius and Utter Illiteracy* (2003). That same year I also saw Andreas Hykade's student film *We Lived in Grass*, which was miles ahead of almost everything else being made at that level.

One of my big flaws back then was quantity. I programmed too much. Sometimes 10–12 special screenings on top of five competition screenings and Panorama. Too much for audiences, too much for our budget.

When I took over selection I made the same mistake—85–90-minute screenings. Now we cap at 75, and honestly 60 would be better. My over-programming—rooted in insecurity and wanting to please—nearly wrecked the festival. When Kelly came back in, she made me cut it way down. A lot of young festivals make the same mistake.

Well, OIAF96 went well and got positive reviews. I'd maybe hoped to rest on my laurels a bit after a relatively successful OIAF '96; instead, I had to jump right in and start creating this brand-new Ottawa International Student Animation Festival (SAFO) that we would debut in the fall of 1997.

We held SAFO—mistakenly—at the NAC, and it did okay, but not great. The NAC was definitely not the venue for it. It was far too big for a festival that was more modest in size than the OIAF. We learned fast, and, for the remaining three SAFO editions, we shifted it to a smaller venue.

Today, I'd never do a student festival, let alone have a separate student competition (e.g., Annecy separates their student films from the main competition). Even though I find that student works can be far more exciting and bold than the more established filmmakers, we can barely find 10–15 student films we can really stand behind. Last year I was on a student-jury for a festival and it was, frankly, pretty underwhelming. The quality just isn't there most years to justify a separate competition, let alone a student festival (unless that festival is solely for students and schools).

The most important part of SAFO97 was that it gave a real platform to young animators. There are folks who went on to have successful careers in animation as filmmakers and teachers: Ülo Pikkov (still making films; now head of animation at the Estonian Academy of the Arts), Fran Krause (CalArts), Brooke Keesling (Bento Box, Netflix), Christy Karacas (co-creator of *Superjail!*, RISD), Jessica Borutski (Ottawa-born; later at Nickelodeon and redesigned the original *Looney Tunes* characters for Warner Bros.), Lorelei Pepi (Emily Carr), Andreas Hykade (Filmakademie Baden-Württemberg), Suzie Templeton.

SAFO97 also let me try selection on my own. We didn't have the budget for a committee, and I wanted to see if in-house selection could work. I didn't do it completely alone—one or two colleagues sat in to help me weed things down—but overall I liked it, and I tried to keep it light. Back then I kept notes on each film; eventually I stopped. If a film resonates, you remember it. No need to overthink it or to use those goofy 1–10 systems. This is subjective work. If it isn't subjective for you, maybe this isn't your line of work.

IMAGE 3.5 Scan of SAFO97 program book cover

Fear not, I'm not going to drag you through every single OIAF. But these early years were all trial and error, and they set up the version of the festival that emerged in the early 2000s.

OIAF98 was, in many ways, utter chaos.

On the bright side, Kelly gave birth to our first son, Jarvis, the morning after our selection committee (the second-last one we ever had) arrived. I was going back and forth between selection screenings and the hospital. Any rational

IMAGE 3.6 OIAF98

person would have had someone else oversee the committee and stayed at the hospital. I suspect I was scared of being a father and, honestly, compassion and selflessness don't come naturally to me. I was trying too hard to prove myself at this job while I was flailing in every other part of my life.

During the festival, we dealt with a stream of crap: a belligerent jury member (that's as far as I'm going with that) and some of the most challenging staff issues we've ever had. To make it worse, I was drinking heavily to deal with work, family, and unresolved paternal stuff (at 15 I learned the man I thought was my father wasn't). I was out of whack. I'm not even sure knowing I was on the autism spectrum would've helped much. I was a mess making bad choices. If anything in here is useful, let it be this: don't do what I did. I've grown, but I still have to live with those selfish choices.

Staffing was always hit and miss. We relied heavily on a government programme (JCP). We were paid to give unemployed people training in a new area. Great idea. But you were limited to whoever was eligible, so it was a roll of the dice every year. And JCPers had mandatory hours off to look for other work, so just when you finished training someone, they'd get a job and disappear. We had our share of oddballs—someone left for lunch and never came back, someone went to a casino and never came back, someone was offended we didn't have a yoga area.

Overall, though, JCP was and is a good programme. It helps people pivot. We still use it, and a bunch of those folks became core CFI/OIAF staff.

Which brings me to 1998, when things tipped over. We had someone helping with sponsorship on a commission basis. I hoped that would motivate them and get us beyond animation companies. It didn't. They wanted to work remotely, weren't producing, always had excuses. Just before—maybe right as—OIAF '98 started, I had to fire them.

Then our guest-services person, who had the hardest job in the building, messed up flights, which cost us money, and also clashed with guests. Then a JCPer running special events melted down at a sponsored party and pissed off the venue and sponsor. I had to fire him in a hotel lobby at midnight. He was already an odd guy—the same clothes, lots of sick days, mystery vibe. While I was trying to fire him, a volunteer kept interrupting. I asked him to go. He didn't. I was burned out and half-drunk and finally snapped and chased him out of the lobby and down Albert Street. Neither of them came back.

1999 was my first rock bottom. We were supposed to run the second SAFO that October. Then August happened. I found the number for the man who was probably my biological father and called him from the office. I have never shaken like that in my life. A week or two later the Arts Court called—there'd been a fire. I biked over. The office looked like a Lynch installation: black everywhere, lights drooping, everything wrecked.

Kelly put it perfectly:

> The CFI basically lost everything. A monitor caught fire and torched the office. Plastic light covers were hanging like stalactites. We saved some stuff, but everything smelled like smoke. Even now, you pull an old file and there's soot on it.[3]

Not long after that I was sitting in the office and suddenly felt very unwell—light-headed, heart pounding, my whole body flushed. I left the office thinking a walk would help, but it just got worse. I almost went into a shop to ask them to call an ambulance. I was sure it was a heart attack or stroke and that this was the end. I went back to the office and asked a colleague to take my car and drive me to the hospital. They ran tests and quickly said everything was fine and that I'd had a panic attack. Up until that moment I thought "panic attack" was just some insane thing kids said to each other when they were noticed by a boy or girl they liked… but no, this is a real medical thing. Looking back, it was pretty damn obvious. Heavy drinking, terrible insomnia, an office fire, personal chaos—yeah, my body finally said, "enough." I had two more of those and that was it, except for a couple of mild ones over a decade later.

IMAGE 3.7 SAFO99

Most incredibly, we held SAFO99 and it actually went okay. But by the end, something had to give. Our producer for OIAF98 and SAFO99 had rightly had enough of working with me and my discombobulated daily state. I think her last words to me were that I should see a therapist. She was right.

After the festival, I sat down with Tom McSorley and proposed hiring the only person who could handle the OIAF and me: Kelly. Our son, Jarvis, was just over a year old and she was itching to get back to work.

And this was a job she already knew inside and out. Even during the years she wasn't working for us, she was volunteering or noticing things the producer had forgotten. Kelly's upbeat and calm personality was perfect for a high-stress event, plus she knew how to deal with me.

For OIAF00, she returned as festival producer while I remained, in name, Executive Director.

Things got better; I didn't. After returning from a visit to Philadelphia to interview Paul and Sandra Fierlinger (both recovering alcohol abusers), I came back to Ottawa feeling even worse about my own state. My brilliant solution was to go to a bar, get into a fight, and wake up with a concussion and a severely broken ankle. When I arrived home, Kelly was so furious that she put a bag of frozen peas on my grotesque ankle and went to sleep. I eventually spent a few days in the hospital. While I slowed the drinking down, I was still a wreck, and during OIAF00 I berated Kelly in front of people for not leaving our social spot, Chez Ani, open for guests who didn't like loud parties. Utterly shameful behaviour. Again, I write this stuff because it's part of the history, it's part of the story, and I see no reason to sweep it under a rug and repaint my years in animation as some bullshit list of highlights.

In 2001, Kelly (yes, she should have left me already!) and I agreed on new roles. I'd step back to part-time and become the Artistic Director, letting me use my strengths and focus on the work I enjoyed. She would become the Managing Director and oversee the OIAF's administration. I cannot say I made many smart decisions in those days, but this was one of the best—it probably saved me, and it definitely saved the OIAF.

To this day, I've always been seen as the face of the OIAF—for better or worse—but the truth is it's nothing without Kelly. She came in and stabilized the place, got the debt I created sorted out, and within a few years, when we had a major organizational crisis, she came up with initiatives that really turned the place around. In 2000, there were just the two of us, but by the end of that decade, we had a full-time team of about a half-dozen people, a new industry event, and a stronger connection with government sponsors, local studios, and the animation industry in general.

The other smart decision I made that year was to stop drinking.

NOTES

1. https://www.awn.com/mag/issue1.10/articles/robinson1.10.html
2. https://www.awn.com/mag/issue1.10/articles/robinson1.10.html
3. *40 Years of Ottawa*. Edited by Chris Robinson and Brittney Mumford, self-published, 2016, p. 26.

CHAPTER 4

Changing of the Guards (2000–2026)

Like I said, I don't want to go through each and every OIAF, so this will be the last chapter on all that stuff. We'll just quickly go through some of the memorable highs and lows and adjustments we made as we continued to grow and, well, survive.

Some might think that being one of the oldest and biggest animation festivals around means we've got it easy. That ain't true. Every year we're basically starting from scratch with funders. On the one hand, it feels ridiculous to be treated like any new outfit; on the other, why should OIAF get a free pass? We should have to prove ourselves—otherwise you risk getting complacent. It's like a tenured professor who stops updating the syllabus. Sure, the students change, but I'd be bored out of my skull repeating the same old thing. You've got to keep it fresh—for audiences and for yourselves. That said, some foundational stability would help. And some funding requirements are, frankly, odd—planning programmes three years out or chasing whatever the theme of the moment is.

And there is always this pressure to programme according to certain agendas and, while I understand it to a degree, it always infuriates me because there's something disingenuous about it. It's like when people apologize or ask for forgiveness for something bad they did—others will often accuse them of apologizing only because they got caught. Still don't get what I'm saying? Years ago, I recall a festival issuing a media release

DOI: 10.1201/9781003633181-5

IMAGE 4.1 Kelly and Chris onstage during SAFO03

proudly boasting about having an all-women jury. It felt ridiculous to me. First, it felt like they were patting themselves on the back: "Hey, look at us! Look at how forward-thinking we are!" My personal feeling is: just shut up and do it. Don't boast about it.

And let me be clear that, for example, Indigenous and LGBTQ+ programming and voices are essential. The question for me is how we present them. I lean toward weaving voices together rather than siloing them. Separate spotlights can be useful and celebratory, but if that's the only tool, you risk turning "inclusion" into a side room instead of the main hall.

And this isn't just me talking—over the years, several of my colleagues (and our staff has long been mostly women, which I realize sounds like that ol' "some of my best friends are…" line, but it's true!) told me they were fed up with women-centric programmes; they found them tokenizing and, weirdly, insulting—as if they were being cordoned off rather than included.

In Ottawa, we've always aimed for balance—on juries, on stages, in conversations—long before it became a talking point. And yes, I am the central decision-maker on selections, but my colleagues, who all come from different backgrounds, generations, and gender identities, have strong input as well. Yet we certainly never issued media releases. Why would we? It just seems like shameful pandering.

We're not looking for quotas; we're looking for the most resonant work. Background and identity matter—context matters—but the work has to lead. We won't programme anything hateful, obviously. At the same time, we're not going to tick boxes just to tick them; that helps no one and it dilutes the programme.

Canada has quotas and expectations we respect, and luckily Canadian work is generally strong. We also created Canadian Panorama and the Canadian Student Competition to keep supporting a wide range of local voices (we're funded in part by Canadian taxpayers, after all). My hope is simple: a lineup where different perspectives stand shoulder to shoulder, and the best work—whoever made it—rises because it's undeniable.

And I'm not remotely suggesting that the OIAF approach is flawless. Our World Panorama selection, for example, could be better. Too often it's been very European-flavoured. The Panorama programme, which at times has shifted to being a sort of "best of the rest," was actually created specifically to provide space for countries and voices that were underrepresented—whose work was, let's be honest, not strong enough for a competition but still merited being shown. That's something we drifted away from and need to return to.

—

Speaking of tricky issues around race and identity, back in 1998 I ran into a situation that really rattled me. Our committee had selected a Polish student film, *Black Burlesque*, by Tomasz Kozak. You can't find it anywhere now, but it was a roughly hand-drawn, caricature-based film that included cliché big-nosed Jewish figures and, I think, a Hitler caricature. The committee selected it, and the jury even gave it an award.

One audience member, though, objected to the film and reported it to two Jewish organizations. One of them was very polite and just asked to get in touch with the director. The other was not polite at all—they were aggressive. They insisted the film was antisemetic and demanded not only that we apologize for showing it but that we change our rules to say we would not accept any hate-driven films.

IMAGE 4.2 Chris Landreth and Ryan Larkin accept the OIAF04 Grand Prize for "Ryan"

I responded with an articulate essay from a member of the selection committee arguing that the film was actually criticizing elements of contemporary Polish society that remained intolerant and closed-minded. They wouldn't hear it. Instead, they escalated and said they could take it to the hate-crimes division of the Toronto police.

I was furious and stressed, but we didn't need the whole thing turning into a public fight. In the end, we sent a pretty half - hearted apology letter, and that was that—all because of one person's complaint.

I've written about the Ryan Larkin story in another book, but let's do a quick summary here because it was a big part of my experiences and definitely played a role in my decision to toss aside alcohol in 2001.

In the summer of 2000, a colleague heard from a friend that a former Oscar-nominated animator was panhandling on the streets of Montreal. I learned this name was Ryan Larkin and he had indeed been nominated in 1968 for his film, *Walking.* I got this idea that maybe we should go to see him and see if we can help him get on his feet again. One weekend, a few of us drove to Montreal and very quickly found Ryan as he was getting ready to start his "shift." He did his panhandling outside of Montreal's famous Schwartz's Deli and I guess Ryan and some others shared a schedule.

Ryan's shift started at 4 p.m. We met him, introduced ourselves, and asked if we could take him to dinner. He was reluctant because he'd miss out on his earnings for the evening (something like $40. Actually he made a decent living except that it all went to alcohol). We gave him $40 and spent the evening eating, drinking, playing pool as he shared stories about his life. He seemed to really want to get back into animation. I suggested he attend the OIAF '00 festival as a guest so that he could just hang out and get a feel for things and maybe meet some folks. He agreed. Later I went even further and suggested he come and sit with what would be our last selection committee (they only judged the commissioned films as I'd taken over selecting the other categories). Again, he agreed, so we brought him over that summer. On that committee were Pjotr Sapegin, Andrei Svislotski (who sadly took his own life in 2022), and Chris Landreth (another Oscar-fêted animator). Landreth got to know Larkin during that week and then in September at the festival proposed making a film about Larkin. This would become the 2004 Oscar winner (and OIAF Grand Prize winner), *Ryan*.

By the time 2004 rolled around though I'd had enough of Ryan. I had been warned by an National Film Board (NFB) veteran not to get involved, but I arrogantly thought my experience would be different. I was wrong. Ryan didn't want to change. He just used people. Typical addict behaviour more than a comment on Ryan personally. On top of that some rather disturbing news was sent to me about Ryan's past misbehaviours. By now, people were hailing Larkin as this great animation figure and I just felt sick because I knew the darkness others didn't. In the end I deeply regretted "discovering" him. I felt Chris was using him, I was using him (the OIAF got nationwide media coverage in 2004), and, well, he was using us. The NFB was using it all. In the end, I wrote a book about it all (*Ballad of a Thin Man*), one that I regret writing and have no desire to revisit.

—

Alright, let's get into this long-standing story/myth about our rejection of Alexander Petrov's *The Old Man and The Sea (1999)*.

Back in 2000, everyone was talking about the film. It was a Russian/Canadian co-production made for IMAX, based on Hemingway's story, and highlighted Petrov's stunning oil-on-glass technique, painting with his fingertips. Technically, it was a pretty astonishing piece of work. By the time it came our way, it had already picked up the Public and Grand Prize at Annecy, an award at Zagreb, and then the Academy Award for Best Animated Short Film. In other words, it arrived with a full suitcase of prestige.

I had actually co-written an in-depth piece for AWN on the making of the film. We spoke with Petrov and with the Montreal producer, Pascal Blais, about the technical challenges, and I even went back and re-read Hemingway's book. My memory of that period is that, once I revisited the novella, I felt the film didn't quite get to the heart of the relationship and tension in Hemingway. So, in what was otherwise a kind of "let's-talk-about-this-amazing-technique" article, I didn't hold back on the narrative side.

Here's the gist of what I wrote back then (about 25 years ago):

> While a friendship developed, a great film did not on a narrative level. For all the hype surrounding *The Old Man and The Sea*, Petrov's vision is a disappointment. Certainly it is difficult to condense Hemingway's novella into a 22-minute film, but within that time Petrov should have explored the complexity of at least one of the old man's relationships (eg. the boy, the marlin, his decaying hands, the sharks, his identity). The struggle between Santiago and the marlin is the backbone of the novel and the film fails to convey the intensity of that relationship. Time spent on, for example, the arm wrestling match in Casablanca could have instead been invested in the battle between the man and fish. In focusing on the non-essentials of the narrative, Petrov's interpretation becomes congested and ultimately superficial. In the novel, the on-going tension is a character in itself, but it is almost entirely absent in the film. In its place is composer Normand Rogers distracting, melodramatic score that serves as an inadequate substitute for the narrative's emotional void. The acting in both the English and French versions of the film are weak. In particular Gordon Pinsent's (a Canadian icon) unemotional impersonation of a Canadian maritime fisherman seems far removed from the shores of Cuba. Beyond the debate of content (and ultimately the scope of this article), one questions whether Petrov's technique is being misused on the construction of natural or photographic-like realism rather than exploring the more creative options of animation.[1]

And that's really the point that has never changed: it was a technical marvel that, for us at Ottawa, didn't land on a narrative level. So we didn't put it into competition. Instead, we offered to place it in the Canadian Panorama.

As I remember it, that didn't go over especially well on the production side. I recall getting a call from Pascal Blais—this is a long time ago, so I won't pretend to remember every word—but my impression was that he was frustrated. Which, honestly, I understood: here was a film that had just won Annecy and the Oscar, and there was an expectation that Ottawa would be the final stop in that run. On my end, I stayed pretty calm—probably because I'd already laid out my thinking in the AWN piece—and I explained what I always explain: the OIAF doesn't make programming decisions based on what other festivals or awards bodies have done. We look at the film and decide whether it fits *our* competition. I also said something like, "You wouldn't really want us to program films just because other people liked them," because that's not a festival, that's a scoreboard.

In the end, the Panorama placement was declined, so the film didn't screen at Ottawa. Apart from a small commercial piece (which I think we did show), Petrov didn't submit to the OIAF after that.

This also wasn't the first time things got a bit tangled between Ottawa and that circle. Back in 1996, the selection committee viewed *The Old Lady and the Pigeon* by Sylvain Chomet, on which Blais was an associate producer. What we saw then was unfinished, and the committee's position was simply that they couldn't fairly judge an incomplete film, so it was disqualified on that basis. Years later I heard that what eventually reached Chomet was the message that Ottawa had "rejected" the film, and understandably he wasn't thrilled. That's how those wires can get crossed in festival land. When I met Chomet at Bucheon International Animation Festival (BIAF) in Korea in 2016, we finally had a chance to talk it through, and I was able to explain what actually happened from our side—that it was about the state of the film, not about him.

So there you go, kids. That's the whole Petrov story as I remember it. Over time the myth made it a bigger, juicier drama than it really was, but I've told it over the years because it's a clean example of what Ottawa has always valued: you can dazzle us with technique—and we love that—but if the film itself doesn't move us, we're not going to put it in competition just because everyone else did.

On a more positive and trivial note, let's quickly talk about posters and signal films. Prior to 2001, with maybe a couple of exceptions, I thought our posters were mediocre. I quickly learned that animators don't necessarily make the best poster designers. At that time, I'd admired the

IMAGE 4.3 Dave Cooper's poster for OIAF02

posters of the Holland Animation Film Festival run by my friend, Gerben Schermer. He used graphic artists like Art Spiegelman and Chris Ware. The posters were just fantastic—beautifully designed and detailed.

Well, things changed for us in 2001, when a young Ottawa graphic artist named Dave Cooper came to the office and asked to do a poster. I said, "Why not." In the end, Dave made posters for SAFO01 and OIAF02. He completely elevated our poster quality and had me seeking different directions in the future for poster designers. From that point on, our posters were, for the most part, the best in OIAF history, as we had talented artists like Gary Baseman, Oscar Grillo, Gary Panter, Howie Tsui, Wong Ping, Elise Simard, Andrea Stokes, and Seth all have a go (though Matthew Rankin's 2023 designs and signal film—inspired by Canadian government designs of the 1970s and 1980s—remain my favourite).

Commissioning the poster and signal film is always tricky because we just don't have much of a budget for them. We really rely on the artist's generosity. If they're connected to a company, we'll offer them an OIAF sponsorship. With that in mind, once I've settled on an artist, I just trust them to make the best work they can. It's like with a jury: you're picking people you respect, who you know would be an asset. For the poster and film, I ask them to include the obvious (dates, name) and, beyond that, I just ask that they include an owl somewhere in the work. I don't care what the owl looks like because I want it to be in their style and voice. When the Hong Kong artist, Wong Ping, made our 2022 poster, I had no clue where the owl was at first. It was so abstract. But that's fine—that's what we want.

Maybe once or twice I had to give some feedback about something that I felt needed adjustment, but for the most part, the biggest battles I have are with my OIAF colleagues, who are always concerned about our look or branding that year and want images they can adapt easily for marketing and promotion.

Seeing the poster for the first time remains the unofficial beginning of that festival. It's the first born, so to speak. That's when you really start to get a sense of the identity for that year.

The only time we ever had a controversy about a poster came in 2009. Theodore Ushev created the poster. It had been loosely inspired by a mishap on a picnic bus the year before, when an attendee projectile vomited, and Ushev was, unfortunately, the recipient of a few chunks.

It started when Sheridan College instructor Pete Emslie openly criticized the poster on his blog (the original post has since been removed). There was some initial back-and-forth between Emslie, Ushev, and me, but it wasn't that big a deal—just different tastes. Then Amid Amidi, over at the online publication *Cartoon Brew*, picked up the story and whaled on Emslie. The story picked up even more steam. Here's an excerpt from the *Cartoon Brew* article:

> The poster was drawn by Theo Ushev, who, in addition to being an accomplished fine artist, is the director of amazing animated shorts

IMAGE 4.4 Theodore Ushev's "Controversial" OIAF09 POSTER

like *Drux Flux* and *Tower Bawher.* In his post, Emslie describes it as 'blecchh!,' a 'cat vomiting,' and writes that its proper place would be 'taped to a fridge door by some loving mom.' It's downright embarrassing to think that this guy represents the quality of instruction and critical thinking at a school that purports itself to be one of the top animation institutions in the world.

> Emslie's criticisms—if describing something as 'blecchh' can be regarded as a valid criticism—drew a response from Ottawa festival director Chris Robinson, who wrote on his blog: 'What annoys me is the infantile hostility coming from a man who claims to have 30 years' experience in animation as an animator and, egad, a teacher (I thought teachers are supposed to be guides. They introduce students to a diversity of possibilities and then let them go off and develop their own thoughts.). This guy doesn't even try. It's just outright reaction. The work is ugly and pretentious and that's that. There's no processing, no attempt to contemplate and consider. He doesn't even encourage dialogue (isn't that one of the primary functions of being a teacher?).'[2]

Later in the article, Amidi wrote:

> At the end of the day, life goes on. Sheridan students who are too young to know any better will continue accepting instruction from a guy who draws cartoon characters on a par with Chris Hart and throws in some tired Hirschfeld impersonations to boot. Theo Ushev will continue making beautiful films and drawings. The Ottawa International Animation Festival will be a great time for everybody who attends. And animation will continue to advance as an art in spite of those who wish to impose primitive rules and restrictions about what a piece of animation can and can't be.[3]

Looking back, the whole thing was ludicrous, but, hey, it was great promotion for the OIAF and it actually generated some healthy—and sometimes silly—conversations about festival posters.

—

Alright, speaking of changes, we've always tinkered with our competition categories. Back in 1992, the categories were things like: Best Production Under 10 Minutes; Best Production Between 10–30 Minutes; Best First Film; Best Student Film; Best Educational Production; Best Children's Animated Production; Animation Productions Especially Produced for a Television Series; and Animation Productions Especially Produced for Television but Not Part of a Series. By OIAF 2025, that had shifted a lot. We didn't just rename things—we split them into separate competitions: Short Film (narrative, non-narrative, student, commissioned), Animated

Feature, Animated Series, Films for Young Audiences 7+, Films for Teens, and the Canadian Student Competition.

I always loathed those early '90s categories. They were so damn wordy. Why not just say "Best Animated TV Series" and "Best Animated TV Special"? And dividing shorts by running time always felt dull and overly specific. Imagine winning and having to say, "Well, yeah, I won… for films between 10–30 minutes."

One ongoing headache has been the non-narrative category—sometimes called Experimental or Abstract. We were never quite sure what to call it, and that uncertainty was mostly because the films themselves kept changing. We always felt it was an important stream to celebrate. The problem is that narrative work has gotten more layered and non-linear, and most so-called non-narrative films have at least a trace of narrative. Ryō Orikasa's OIAF award winners, *Miserable Miracle* (2023 Grand Prize for Best Short) and *The Graffiti* (2025 award for Best Narrative), for example, could slide either way. That's why we try things, rename things, split things, fold things back in—if it doesn't work, we change it. No harm done. Some days I think: maybe we should just have one main short-film category.

For years I fought against having competition screenings for children. Animation is already mislabeled as "for kids," and I wanted to push back on that. Eventually I softened, and honestly, having a kids' jury—an idea I pinched from my former colleague at Animafest Zagreb, Buba Antauer, who told me how great it was to have kids judging—has become one of the festival's highlights. You never know what they'll say on stage.

But you do have to remember they're there. One year, a staffer put together the winner clips and I wasn't watching the screen. Suddenly I saw parents and kids filing out, shooting me dirty looks. I asked, "Did I miss something?"—which only annoyed them more. Turned out there were drawings of penises in the clip. Parents confronted us afterwards. I thought they overreacted—these were drawings, and, come on, half their kids were probably doodling the same thing in school notebooks.

In 2024, the screw-up was mine. We were honouring British animator Emma Calder, who had just passed away, and I decided we should show her last film, *Beware of Trains*, before the awards. I'd forgotten about the raunchy sex scenes. I went back onstage apologizing right away… and those parents just laughed and made jokes about therapy bills. Much better crowd.

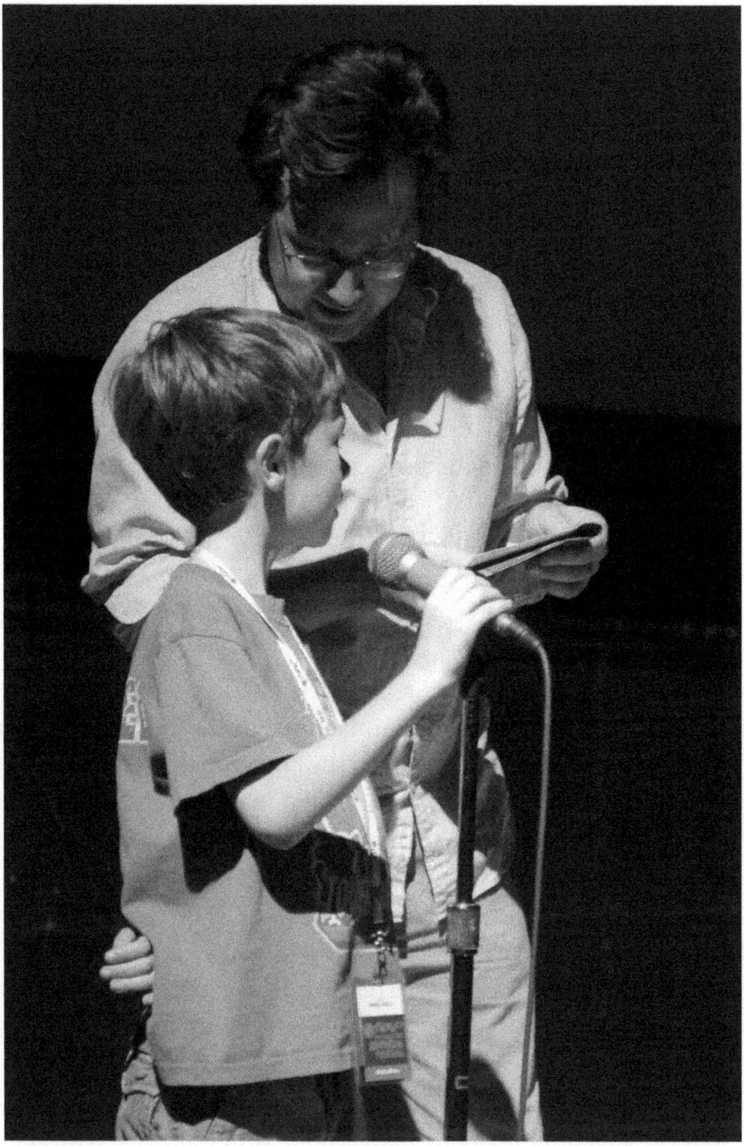

IMAGE 4.5 Chris and son Jarvis introducing at OIAF07 screening

The point is we've never been afraid to change categories. You have to stay flexible. In the early 2000s we even added films made for the internet—little Flash films made specifically for online viewing. As the line between "internet" and "regular" shorts disappeared, so did the need for that category.

In 2002, we introduced an Animated Feature category (Richard Linklater's *Waking Life* won the first Grand Prize). I'm still not 100% sure it was a good idea. Back then it was hard to even find three decent features—I always set three as the minimum to justify a category. Now there are plenty. But opening the door to features also brought more of a live-action mindset. Distributors submit the film and agree to our clearly stated artist fees ... then, once they're accepted, they start demanding theatrical rates. We don't play that game. We put our energy into filmmakers who actually want the film shown.

Since we're on features: premieres. I hate that whole racket. I get that it can help with distributors and buzz, but it's often bad for filmmakers and festivals. Thankfully, OIAF never really had to play that game. We rarely mention premieres. Audiences don't come for the word "premiere"—they come for the film.

Another game I won't play: "This film already won somewhere fancy, so we should select it." Good for you if you won at Annecy or the Oscars, but that's not a reason for us to take it. That's lazy programming. Pick the films you actually like.

In 2004 we tried a New Media Competition: internet shorts, internet series, interactive work, and machinima (films made with game software). Machinima was ahead of its time—and the people making it actually came to the festival. But the jury didn't know what to do with it (and maybe my selection didn't help), so they refused to give an award. The filmmakers were...vocal. That was the end of machinima at OIAF.

In the 2020s we briefly had a virtual reality (VR) category. We dropped it. The work wasn't that strong, converting films to VR felt pointless, and watching too much VR during selection made us physical nauseous. More than that, VR and festivals just don't mix—festivals are about shared spaces; VR is the opposite. It's a category I'm glad we tried, but I don't miss it.

We also had a High School category for a while. We opened each Short Competition screening with one high school film. It messed with the flow (yes, I'm precious about that—see Chapter 6), but it gave young filmmakers a real shot. One of them, Gints Zabalodis, from Latvia, made *Priorities*, which won in 2014...,and later made *Flow*, which went on to win 55 awards, including an Oscar and Grand Prizes at Annecy and OIAF. So: sometimes those experiments pay off in ways you don't expect.

The lesson—because I have to pretend this has a lesson—is: be open to new categories, try things, but don't be afraid to kill them if they don't work. And ignore the media's obsession with "what's new this year?" Something is new every year: the films. New artists, new countries, new voices. That's the real novelty.

—

In 2003, we had two big blows. First, the National Arts Centre just up and decided to remove all their projection equipment, so we were instantly without what had been our main Ottawa venue since 1976. Then Telefilm Canada, the main film-funding department of the Canadian government, out of the blue, announced they were cutting funding to virtually every film festival that wasn't TIFF. We were floored. We were screwed.

Serge Losique was still, in name at least, head of our board/organization and, as usual, he was, frankly, not very helpful. He told us to do nothing. Wait it out. Kelly and I ignored him and went on a massive media campaign that ended up driving the Telefilm Canada administrative assistant to tears from all the calls and faxes (Google "fax," kids) that poured in from the international animation community. We had animators like Bill Plympton go on radio shows to sing our praises. We had studios saying they'd step in and help in any way they could. Then we had this amazing local politician, the late Mauril Bélanger, who I spoke to a couple of times, and it was like something out of Watergate. He wouldn't convey much information but assured us that things were in the process of being fixed. And eventually they were and the money was restored (though the NAC projection equipment wasn't). Because of this, two key OIAF initiatives were born.

First, Kelly (with input from our past CFI and OIAF director, Frank Taylor) came up with the idea of having an industry-friendly Television Animation Conference (TAC—though it's now just The Animation Conference). Before that, we were admittedly short on offering the industry much since I was adamant about promoting indie artists. TAC was a great compromise.

While TAC later became associated with two superstar OIAFers and ex–Carleton Film Studies grads, Maral Mohammadian (now a producer at the NFB) and Azarin Sohrabkhani (now at Netflix), who really crafted the conference into something unique, it was Kelly and Frank who came up with it all. It was a great move because it gave industry a bigger space at the OIAF while protecting my weird indie programming corner.

Second, the NAC problem was a bit of a blessing. I was fed up with the place and in 2003, about a dozen film prints were damaged. The NAC did

6/26/03

THAT'S ALL FOLKS

TELEFILM DUMPS OTTAWA ANIMATION FESTIVAL

ANITA GRACE | news

The news hit like a giant mallet to the face. Telefilm Canada was pulling its money out of the Ottawa International Animation Festival, end of story.

"We had absolutely no notice," said the festival's managing director, Kelly Neall. "We were due to receive our funding in a month."

Funding that for more than 20 years has been a financial backbone for the festival, covering about 25 per cent of costs and currently running at $52,000 annually. "They even increased our funding last year," the festival's artistic director Chris Robinson told X Press. "What kind of sign is that?"

So far, there's been little explanation from Telefilm beyond a general statement about a change in policy and only funding projects that will attract a wider audience. It seems 30,000, or the number who attended last year's festival, doesn't fit into their definition of "wide."

Alejandra Sosa, who handles the Animation Festival file from the Telefilm office in Toronto isn't speaking with reporters and would tell Robinson only that the cuts are part of the corporation's strategy. But Douglas Chow in Telefilm's Montreal office told X Press the cuts were part of a "new corporate objective ... to build audiences and help support the creation of cultural productions with box office potential."

"We all know what that means," said Robinson. "Men with Brooms II."

Ottawa's biennial festival — it alternates with the Ottawa International Student Animation Festival, being held this year in October — was launched in 1976, is the second largest in the word and the only one of its kind in North America. The next festival was scheduled for September 2004, but Robinson said they will be out of money by November.

Telefilm insists the cut has been public knowledge for over a year and that the industry knew it was coming but Robinson wonders which part of the industry they're referring to.

Animation producers are just as baffled. "Why would the government want to get rid of something that has such a big following globally?" asked Jason Belec, a vice president at Notarninanimation Studios in Ottawa.

Among participants in last October's festival was local animation wizard Dave Cooper (www.davegraphics.com), whose portfolio includes working on Simpsons' creator Matt Groening's *Futurama*, and who recently toured the U.S. with works displayed at the 2002 event.

"This decision really reveals a total lack of understanding in the art form of Animation," wrote Cooper in an e-mail to X Press. "The vast majority of artists working in the field are making short films. To cut funding to a festival that specializes in short films is tantamount to saying that animation isn't a worthwhile form of expression.

"And just from the point of view of a Canadian artist, the festival has been absolutely invaluable. I've worked in animation for years, almost exclusively for American clients, but it's right here in Ottawa that I've learned the most about not only the art form of animation, but the hard, cold business of it too."

Belec said the Animation Festival was vital for developing young talent, especially those who were looking beyond commercial opportunities. "How else do you get into the industry?" he asked. "There's no way without a festival."

The Animation Festival office was flooded with over 300 letters and e-mails of support from local and even international studios in Italy, Korea, Argentina, Brazil, Estonia and Los Angeles. Robinson said he'd like to dump them on Telefilm headman Richard Stursberg's desk and that they will be used in appeals to Ottawa city councillors, local politicians and the Department of Heritage.

But he concedes the festival's survival depends on more than letters from supporters. They need money, and for that, Robinson's looking to the industry. "If we really are that important to them," he said. "It's time to step up."

Fine, but will the industry be able to fill the gap?

"A lot of us would love to and a lot of us will try to," said Belec. "But we're not exactly rolling in dough." While he predicts growth in the industry, especially in computer animation, he is not sure there would be enough to fund festivals without at least some tax dollar support.

And then there's the catch-22. If a corporation, Hollywood's DreamWorks for example, steps forward as the big sponsor, Belec said, some animators fear it could wrest control of the entire event.

"Corporate sponsorship introduces a whole bunch of new problems which the festival people aren't used to dealing with," said Belec. "They're in a really tight bind."

WE NEVER SAW IT COMING: OTTAWA ANIMATORS FEAR DESTRUCTION OF FESTIVAL

graphic Dave Cooper

IMAGE 4.6 "That's all Folks" – OIAF Funding Cut scandal

an internal investigation—we all know how those always turn out—and found no evidence of wrongdoing. Let's see, films were okay when they arrived at the NAC. Films were not okay when they left the NAC. Hmm… Anyway, for me, it was enough. It was time to get out of this rule-heavy place and find a space that really fit our DIY/indie character.

7/17/03

ANIMATED ABOUT-FACE

Ottawa's animation festival got its money back. But the battle's not over yet.

Telefilm Canada did an about-face last week and announced it would fund the Ottawa International Animation Festival for one more year. Two weeks earlier, Telefilm suddenly announced it was cutting its annual $52,000 contribution, which makes up a critical 25 per cent of the festival's costs.

But the toon-fest refused to roll over into the grave Telefilm dug for them. Organizers came out with both barrels loaded and blazed away in Technicolor.

"I think we caught Telefilm off guard," said the festival's artistic director, Chris Robinson. "None of the other festivals that got cut unleashed an attack like we did."

Robinson's crew took copies of the 300-plus letters of support — including some from animators at Walt Disney and Dreamworks and independents in Estonia, Finland and Colombia — and dumped them on Telefilm desks. They made similar deliveries to Mayor Bob Chiarelli and Heritage Minister Sheila Copps. Ottawa-Vanier MP Mauril Bélanger was also recruited into the fight.

It worked. Douglas Chow, Telefilm's taciturn communications rep, would only confirm that the federal government's film-support agency had received the letters, not that they influenced the decision. "We listened to the festival's concerns about funding cuts and responded accordingly," is all he said.

Chow would not speculate about the future of Telefilm's relation to animation, but said consultations will be held with the industry.

Robinson has little enthusiasm for consultations with Telefilm, and said even this funding reprieve doesn't mean the festival is out of the woods.

"It's been a wake-up call," he said. Some money has come from the private sector, but Robinson said the industry will have to step up if they want the festival to continue.

The Ottawa International Animation Festival is the largest in North America and draws 30,000 spectators each year.

ANITA GRACE

IMAGE 4.7 "Animated About-Face" – OIAF Funding restored

In 2004, the ByTowne Cinema took over as our main screening venue and remains that to this day. I love the ByTowne. Kelly and I had a long history there. She worked there for a number of years and I was a frequent visitor. The place has a character and aura—it's right in a part of town with a few shelters, so you see a wider mix of people around—that just fits the OIAF like a glove. And their staff are just amazing. The staff are fantastic—people who love film and care about their venue and audience. We had a brief scare during the pandemic when it looked like the ByTowne might close, but thankfully some young guys from Toronto came in and really made the place successful again.

"Some people were disappointed we stopped being at just one venue, but times changed and that venue just didn't have the tech we needed," said Kelly in 2016. "We also had a great deal of trouble fitting into their schedule. The current group of venues, though, are all within walking distance—and work quite well."[4]

And since we're talking about downtown: OIAF attendees are sometimes surprised by how many unhoused and clearly struggling people are in that part of Ottawa. That's not a vibe problem, it's a systems problem. The vast majority of those folks aren't a threat; they're just trying to get through the day. What frustrates me is that our health and social services—municipal, provincial, federal—keep talking about mental health, trauma, addiction, housing, and then the practical "solution" on the street ends up being a pop-up police station. And we all know the last people qualified to deal with complex mental health crises are police.

I also don't get the planning logic: this is a tourist-heavy part of the city, it's where our venues are, and it's also where several shelters and community spaces are clustered. So people come downtown once a year for the festival and think Ottawa is a city of broken people. Ottawa isn't uniquely broken; it's just where governments chose to concentrate people with nowhere else to go—and then underfund the supports that would actually help.

It's strange that despite being sober from 2001 to 2011, I can barely recall much about the OIAF editions during that time. To a degree, sobriety made it more difficult for me because I do not naturally socialize with people. Alcohol loosened me up during festivals. Without that aid, I really struggled (not that I regret that choice one bit). Certainly writing was dominating my life more and there were periods when my interest in the OIAF was waning. You don't spend 35 years at a job and not have periods of doubt and bouts of boredom. Plus, being fully annual (even though we were doing annual since 1996), once one festival passed, you forgot it and moved on. In fact, in the weeks leading up to one festival I'd already be working on programming for the following year's edition (much to the annoyance of my colleagues).

In 2006, Kelly was home with our second son, Harrison. I had pleaded with her to let me oversee the festival while she was away. I wanted a

IMAGE 4.8 The Inaugural TAC in 2004

chance at redemption. I wanted to prove to her, my colleagues, and myself that I could do that job I bungled in the late 1990s.

Big mistake. Other than starting this new initiative with the awful name "Animation Celebration" (free opening-day events for local schools), I was a resounding failure. I can't even explain why today. I guess I'm just not built for certain jobs. Because of that dumb decision, it meant more work for my colleagues (who are already overworked and underpaid), and even Kelly kept on working here and there.

Then it got worse. I hit a second "rock bottom" between 2009 and 2012. In late 2008, my oldest and closest friend, Barry Doyle, dropped dead at age 41. It sent me into an almost comatose state of depression for more than a year. It was just awful. I was lying in bed, sobbing. I don't even want to expand on it. It was just terrible. At the end of that year, my grandmother, who had raised me for the first chunk of my childhood, died. Okay, she had been in a zombie-like state for years because of Alzheimer's, so the death was a bit of a relief to our family, but on the heels of Barry's death I just got deeper and deeper into my own zombie state.

IMAGE 4.9 Kelly with newly born, Harrison at OIAF06

Then in early 2010, I had an unnecessary cancer scare because of my damn dentist, but somehow it was prescient because at the end of that year I did in fact have cancer. 2011–2012 was just awful: biopsies, surgeries, chemotherapy, and Kelly and I split. To make matters worse, the whole experience broke me mentally, physically, and emotionally, and in 2012 I had what I guess would be called a nervous breakdown. It was so bad that I was almost forced out of the festival. To this day, I can never forget the compassion that Tom and especially Kelly (who had taken so much shit from me) showed me that year. Just writing and thinking about it now is difficult.

The one edition I will certainly never forget was OIAF11. In September 2011, I'd just moved into my own apartment. That was tough with two sons and the end of an almost 20-year relationship. At the same time, I'd been placed on surveillance by my doctor. Following a biopsy and retroperitoneal lymph node dissection (RPLND)—a major surgery that involved them going in and basically turning your stomach/abdomen area upside down as they removed potentially malignant lymph nodes (they found a few)—it was decided to put me on surveillance (which involved regular tests to keep track of things). Everything was fine all summer but two weeks before OIAF11, I got a call at the office. The cancer was back. Chemotherapy was scheduled for the morning of September 26, the day after the festival ended.

I look back and now it's still emotional. I was in a terrible mental space. Making it worse (though that wasn't the intent!) was our Honorary President David Verrall. He'd been a long-standing producer and executive producer at the National Film Board of Canada. An absolutely lovely man. He took the stage twice that year at the opening and closing. In each speech, he mentioned me a lot and talked about having a cabinet filled with notes from NFB colleagues complaining about me (there was a time I'd have been punched if I ventured to their building).

There was a period where I was very loud in the media and even at an NFB conference about the problems I saw with the organization. Anyway, David talked about how people were very unsure of me when I took over the OIAF but how over time he saw that I did know what I was doing and that I had a vision. I really don't remember it all but he said the nicest things and I was definitely in tears... it really did feel like I was at my own memorial. I vividly remember the closing night. I remember snapping at Azarin for no good reason. I was just a mess. I remember desperately not wanting the festival to end because I thought I'd end.

The best gift that year was the debut of Joel Frenzer as our sort of master of ceremonies (more on that later).

That brings us to 2020. I'm sure there were other years worth mentioning (like when Phil Mulloy won the Grand Prize for Best Animated Feature for a third time and some people actually booed—a first at the OIAF; I'm sure Phil secretly loved it.), but for me the pandemic period will remain one of the strangest, saddest, and somehow most loving periods.

We all know what unfolded between 2020 and 2022. And I believe the OIAF was one of the few festivals that was held fully online twice. Much of it is still a blur to me. I was very doubtful about the whole idea of doing a festival on a computer. We all know what unfolded between 2020 and 2022. And I believe the OIAF was one of the few festivals that was held fully online twice. Much of it is still a blur to me. I was very doubtful about the whole idea of doing a festival on a computer. Back in 2012, Amid Amidi at *Cartoon Brew* asked me why artists should even attend festivals when everything was online. I told him, "That's like saying why have sex when I can jerk off anytime I want to." Somehow though, thanks to Eventive and our amazing technical team of Keltie Duncan and Devin Hartley, OIAF20 came about as close as you can get to capturing the essence of an in-person festival.

IMAGE 4.10 Chris and the online OIAF20 jury of Wong Ping, Don McWilliams, and Pixie Cram

We presented the competition films live, with an announcer (as we've always done). The chat groups were open throughout. Initially I feared that the chat room would lead to negative comments or trolls, but it was the complete opposite. The chats oozed love and support. The OIAF attendees are a big part of what makes the festival successful and there's no doubt that it was their positive attitude and energy that made the 2020 and 2021 editions so special. Aside from the talks and screening packages, we had "hangouts" where people just signed in and we all drank and laughed and hung out. The first year in particular was just amazing… probably because everything was so new, people were so isolated, and we were all just desperate for anything to shake us out of this feeling of alienation. During that first year, in what might be an animation festival first, we overlapped with Zagreb. They had held a limited live edition and some of their guests would join the OIAF hangouts.

It was also the year I became legitimized. At the tail end of 2019, I'd been notified by Animafest Zagreb that I was being awarded for my contribution to animation studies. I was mystified yet, sure, it felt good to be acknowledged, but I never feel I deserve these things. And it made perfect sense that the one year I get an award the pandemic would hit and the festival would be cancelled—or in Zagreb's case postponed to September. Obviously I couldn't attend and had to give my acceptance speech from a terrace in Montreal (where I was living during that period.

We were forced to do it all over again in 2021 and it was okay, but by then we were all burnt out by the isolation. I dearly hope we never experience that again.

When I arrived at my first festival in person in late 2021 in Ljubljana (I moonlight for the amazing Animateka festival as a programming consultant and co-host of filmmaker talks), there were a lot of tears. People were just so happy to be with people again. It was so moving. It was the same feeling when OIAF returned in person in 2022. One particular day was one of our most challenging ever. A competition screening was delayed an hour because of a server problem. Flabbergasted, Joel Frenzer and I had to find ways to entertain the crowd. Joel was brilliant at distracting them and involving them. The mood was so special that people almost seemed disappointed when the screening restarted.

Then it got weirder.

Our famous Animators' Picnic had been catered by a local social enterprise for years. It was a great initiative and we never had any issues. I got to the picnic early so that I could sneak in some lunch before the flood of guests arrived. I had some mac and cheese. All was good until a couple of hours later. Just as I'd finished announcing the winners of our annual pumpkin-carving competition, I suddenly felt very nauseous. I immediately jumped on my electric scooter and darted back to my room where, well, I sang a prayer to the porcelain gods.

With the help of Croatian animator and jury member, Marko Tadić, I felt better enough later to introduce the 9 p.m. competition screening. I quickly made a joke: "Anyone have the mac and cheese and maybe not feel so good?" Suddenly a flurry of hands rose. Soon I learned that many folks had been hit with some food poisoning. I remember Wendy Tilby (*The Flying Sailor*) saying that the moment she and Amanda Forbis completed their phone interview with our local radio station, she vomited. Later, Gerben fled the competition screening early, eventually texting me, "I didn't make it." There were so many similar stories: I imagined a festival video montage of assorted vomiting. Looking back now, yes, food poisoning is unpleasant, but the whole thing was pretty damn funny.

Kelly eventually discovered the cause. "It turned out that the culprit was some donated cheese powder, which was unfortunate for everyone involved!"[5]

IMAGE 4.11 Kelly and Chris at OIAF13

I remember eating the meal with my son Jarvis. I asked him later if he got sick. He said, "No, something felt off about it." That was the last year we used that caterer.

But in other years people might've been outraged and made a big stink about it; that year we lucked out. Everyone was just so happy to be in person that they shrugged it off. Even an awkward introvert like me, who struggles in social situations and has to "mask" to get through each OIAF, was moved. It just felt so good being around these animation weirdos.

One downside was that people started expecting festivals to be hybrid. I made it clear once we were back in person that we weren't doing that. You're either at the festival, being part of it, or you're not. There's no in-between.

Hopefully that whole experience put an end to the question of whether we need festivals—or any social events, really. You want to stay home—do that. The rest of us will be out there being.

—

And so, here we are. It's 2026 (I'm guessing, since I'm writing this in late October 2025), and the OIAF turns 50. That's pretty incredible for any

IMAGE 4.12 Chris and 'little' David Cuevas

arts/culture organization. It's a testament to all the people who've worked on and contributed to the OIAF's history—volunteers, staff, filmmakers, attendees, and, hell, Canadian taxpayers.

A lot has changed. For the last three years I've been programming from Cyprus and Ukraine. That simply wouldn't have been possible—or even imaginable—when I first started. We don't mail newsletters or entry forms anymore. Filmmakers just go to the website, fill out the form, and click submit. No more tapes or film prints to unwrap. No more shelves crammed with packages. No more mailing submissions back. I can open every entry with one click.

That said, I do sometimes miss the physical nature of the pre-digital years. And there are days when the software glitches or the platform freezes and I wonder if this is actually easier than "the old days." Spreadsheets make me dizzy; I just can't work with them. I don't have a good explanation, but putting index cards on a wall or building the OIAF schedule on a bulletin board with thumbtacks and paper is far more calming.

These OIAF chapters are written through one person's eyes (though Kelly gave feedback throughout). It's subjective and, naturally, biased. Kelly's version would be different—and just as valid. While this was always intended to be my version of the OIAF, the festival has succeeded because of many people beyond Kelly and me. Over the years—especially since Kelly stabilized the OIAF in the early-to-mid-2000s—staff have contributed enormously to its growth and evolution.

I've already mentioned Maral Mohammadian and Azarin Sohrabkhani, whose work on TAC and the industry side has been essential. Former tech directors André Coutu, Jerrett Zaroski, and Keltie Duncan kept the CFI and OIAF in step with technological change; Keltie was also a key programming collaborator who kept me on my toes. Current staffers like Devin Hartley (Keltie's former assistant, now in that role) and Amanda Misko (who came from the veterinary field to tackle industry programming—her infectious positivity nicely balances Kelly's and my occasional jadedness) have been terrific. Christina Frolova-Gregory has reinvented and modernized our historically erratic media/communications function—long handled by JCPers—which is a tough portfolio to be dropped into.

The OIAF succeeds because it's collaborative. And, not to pat ourselves on the back, but while Kelly and I are in charge, we've stayed open to new ideas and approaches. Not everyone thrives with independence; these folks did—and do.

The festival has also been a training ground. Many staff—like Kelly and me—arrived with no experience and left with skills, confidence, and a solid résumé. There's only so far you can go unless you're in a top role, though. It's a bit like raising a family: eventually the kids grow up, move on, and carve out their own space.

It's not just staff. We've had amazing champions over the last 35 years—from superstar attendees like Pilar Newton and Brent Smith to Scott Dyer and Pat Burns (both early champions of TAC); Linda Simensky, Brooke Keesling, Karl Staven, and Gary Schwartz; to schools like Rhode Island School of Design, MassArt, Sheridan College, Pratt Institute, and most of all the amazing animation department at Algonquin College in Ottawa who've provided the OIAF with a steady stream of amazing volunteers. I could go on and on. It's a long list.

Without these people and institutions, it wouldn't matter what Kelly or I have done.

There are many nice OIAF stories, but let me share two of my favourites.

In the middle of OIAF16 I came down with a bad flu. My throat felt like gravel. I'd dragged myself out of bed to get ready for a Meet the Filmmakers session, which naturally involves a lot of talking. I felt terrible but there was nothing to be done. As I was entering the theatre, I walked past a table where our young and eager volunteer, David Cuevas (who first attended OIAF13 at age 11), was interviewing an animator.

Lightning struck.

David is one of those ferocious cinephiles. I knew he'd been watching all the films and that he had a very curious mind. I asked him if he wanted to co-host the session with me. He didn't hesitate.

It was an instant hit. He was 14 at the time, so his youthful questions were a nice balance to my therapist approach. For the next few years, David continued as a co-host.

IMAGE 4.13 Pilar Newton's impression of the OIAF

In recent years, the now legally of drinking age David has been part of our programming team and working as a jury coordinator. This year he also created his own festival in Ottawa. He's like our adopted OIAF son and it's been fun to watch him grow. I wouldn't be surprised if he took over my job or Tom's in the future.

Oh, and there's no better example of how the OIAF brings people together than the story of former staffer Tina Paas and Neels Britz. During SAFO01 selection, Tina and I chose a film from South Africa for the Panorama screening. Much to my surprise, the young animator travelled all the way to Ottawa to attend. Once here, he met Tina; they eventually fell in love, married, and now have two children and live in Winnipeg. You just never know.

I'm now in my 35th year with the OIAF. I'm not oblivious: my days (and Kelly's) here are getting shorter. I'm approaching my sixth decade, and at some point I'll have to step back and let someone else programme. I keep an eye on people who could take the reins, but I also think I should let it be. The OIAF will, I hope, continue after Kelly and me, and the direction it takes should be up to whoever comes next.

As the OIAF enters its 50th year, the animation industry is going through unprecedented upheavals. The models that used to support festivals like the OIAF are vanishing. In this age where creators are all the more important, I hope we'll find new ways to ensure that the festival continues. As long as the festival keeps its nerve and its curiosity, it should be fine—whoever's steering.

NOTES

1 https://www.awn.com/animationworld/old-man-and-sea-hands-above-rest
2 https://www.cartoonbrew.com/bad-ideas/sheridan-instructor-attempts-art-criticism-and-fails-16178.html
3 https://www.cartoonbrew.com/bad-ideas/sheridan-instructor-attempts-art-criticism-and-fails-16178.html
4 *40 Years of Ottawa*. Edited by Chris Robinson and Brittney Mumford, self-published, 2016, p. 30.
5 Interview with author, November 2025.

CHAPTER 5

Mix Tapes, Andy Kaufman, and the Joy of Disorder

FILM COMPETITIONS ARE SENSELESS. The same can be said of any artistic competition. There is no objectively perfect film or work of art. It's all subjective and biased. Anyone who tells you differently is full of dog droppings. The whole competition thing is a racket, a big con job.

So why do we do it?

Good question. The only reason I can think of is that winning an award potentially helps filmmakers find funding for a new project or maybe land a job doing commercial work or at a studio.

Now let's go back through this whole process. As I said previously, the OIAF commissioned outside selection committees from 1976 until 2000, when we had half committee, half internal selection. Serving as Selection Committee coordinator for OIAF92 and OIAF94 gave me first-hand insight into the mechanics of committees. I disliked it from the start. Too democratic and diplomatic. Compromises made, deals struck. Films selected because of the filmmaker's name more than the quality of the film itself. The other thing that mystified me—probably because I come from a literature/music/film studies background—was the obsession with technique. How a film was made seemed to outweigh what it actually said. Something always rubbed me the wrong way about it all. And I'd feel frustrated and powerless

DOI: 10.1201/9781003633181-6

IMAGE 5.1 Mixed tape

watching them accept films that—for me at least—felt subpar. It also felt like all the festivals looked the same to some degree.

Art is not democratic, so why the hell should we judge it with the cold impotence of the United Nations? Again, it was Gerben Schermer I first started sharing my frustrations with, and he suggested we just scrap the committees and do the selection ourselves. His argument was that a festival should be like a gallery or museum. There should be a curator. There should be an identity, something unique. I completely agreed, but given the OIAF's history and the sense of ownership that some felt toward it, I was hesitant to make that step.

Then came SAFO '97. With a significantly smaller budget than the OIAF, we had no choice but to gut the committee. The experience of overseeing selection for SAFO '97 and SAFO '99 ultimately gave me the confidence to stop with committees entirely after OIAF 2000. But it wasn't just about being some aesthetic "dictator"; it was also about cold, hard cash. Each year, more submissions were arriving. That means you need committee members for longer periods. There were people who were reluctant to take on that much work. They all had jobs and lives. And remember, a festival is covering the cost of flights, hotels, and meals—and then the cost

IMAGE 5.2 Sequencing the competition for OIAF 17

of their flights and hotels for the actual festival along with those of the International Jury. It's a ludicrous amount of money being tossed away that could've been used for more useful parts of the festival.

The first OIAF that was entirely programmed internally was OIAF '02, and it's remained that way ever since.

One of the most frequent questions I get is what I look for in a film. It's both an easy and a complicated answer. My festival colleagues tend to overthink it, taking detailed notes and using numerical voting systems. That just doesn't work for me. If a film resonates, you'll remember it throughout the selection process. And, as I've told people, for me it's simple: do I ever want to see this film again? That might seem superficial, but it's not. Many films are understood after one screening—everything wrapped up neatly, nothing unanswered. That's boring. I want to be a bit confused (in a good way). I want mysteries, but I also want to feel a pull to rewatch and uncover more. The complexity comes from time and ageing. Our identities are fluid. Notions of self, of taste—they change over time. Not in an obvious way—more like dripping molasses. I am not the programmer I was in 2002 or 2012. You might not notice, but I look back and sometimes scratch my head at the decisions I made. Some might see that as a negative; I see it as growth.

People always seem surprised that I watch all the submissions. I'm not sure why. It's my job. I know other artistic directors who only watch a fraction and rely on colleagues to weed things down. That doesn't make sense to me. Yes, of course I do get help later in the process, but I want to be responsible for what's in and what's out. It's not about mistrusting other people; I just feel it's my duty to go through every submission. No, I don't watch every film from start to finish. I'm confident enough to know relatively quickly what works—or doesn't—for us.

Also, because the OIAF has different categories within the Short Film Competition, we can easily divide it up. You're not judging student films against narrative, or non-narrative against commissioned work. At this stage, you're looking for the best in each category.

Our approach is relatively straightforward.

First off, the Animated Features, Series, Young Audiences, and Canadian Student Competitions are generally all set by early June. Usually those decisions are made by me and a few colleagues (especially for the features).

For the Short Film Competition, there are about three rounds:

ROUND 1 (MARCH 1–MAY 31)

I go through every submission. I start the moment we begin receiving them. It's not as overwhelming as you'd think—at least until the last week of May. Animators, to this day, always wait until the last possible minute to submit, even when the film was ready much earlier. For the most part, between March 1 and late May, I'm watching anywhere from 20 to 50 films a day. At this stage, I'm pretty generous. You're really just weeding out the works you know don't fit with the OIAF. If I see a hint of possibility, the film goes to Round 2.

ROUND 2 (ONE WEEK IN MID-/LATE JUNE)

Here we're maybe left with a quarter of the submissions (probably less). Over four to five days, we act more like a traditional selection committee. I meet with two, three, or four colleagues (most of whom have film-programming experience), and each day we go through one of the four short-film categories. Narrative and student categories usually have the biggest piles. I'll give us a ballpark target (e.g., 10–15 commissioned titles).

ROUND 3 (LAST WEEKEND OF JUNE): THE MIX TAPE

At this point, I go off alone with a relatively short list of films. This is where things get a bit different, I guess. This is where the "mix tape" approach comes in. Honestly, for years I never thought of sequencing in those terms. It's possible someone made the comparison to me, or something about the process reminded me of those teenage days on my bedroom floor copying songs I liked onto cassettes. Sometimes it was dictated by the artist or theme, sometimes just a batch of songs I loved at the time. Programming shorts isn't that different: you're thinking about flow, about contrast, about what follows what, about how to keep a viewer awake and curious for 70-odd minutes.

Nothing drives me crazier than attending a competition screening and feeling like no thought was given to the sequencing of the films. Too often they seem randomly placed or dictated by the odd notion that you should never show the same countries or techniques next to each other. Others follow themes. And there are indeed more festivals that construct their competitions around particular themes. Hey, that's fine. At least they're making something unique to them, but for me that's a potentially restrictive and uninteresting approach. Maybe once or twice I've constructed a screening around a theme that I only accidentally discovered after we'd finished Round 2.

As I've written, I got my first taste of sequencing the competition screenings in 1992. Inside our office was a vault. I guess they kept confiscated stuff there when it was a courthouse. Inside we'd have meetings and screenings, but I remember using the outside door to do the sequencing, plastering the door with index cards for each film. It was totally new to me and I don't recall having any particularly strong feelings about it, but over time I started to love it. I recognized the power you had. You could toy with people's emotions. You could start with a film that had people howling with laughter and then quickly switch gears and follow it up with a real tearjerker. One year, there was a new *Wallace & Gromit* film everyone was aching to see. The screening attracted more of the general public than usual. Well, before I ended the screening with that film, I "gifted" them with an absurdist and cryptic 15-minute Estonian film. Hearing the uncomfortable shuffling of bodies and feet in the cinema gave me so much pleasure.

What also made OIAF programming fun was that our competition was unlike any other—and for the most part, still is. We screen narrative, non-narrative, commissioned, and student films all together. Annecy, for example, separates virtually all of those categories into their own

IMAGE 5.3 Selection Committee week at OIAF

competition screenings. The mix of categories at the OIAF made the sequencing all that much more fun. You could use commercials or music videos to break up the heavier films.

As a side note: I always loved (especially when we used to include TV episodes in the competition, something we stopped because TV episodes are too long and their tone is loud, fast, and really at odds with the overall tone of indie films) observing people from industry and indie worlds having to sit together and tolerate each other's works.

One of my fondest moments was during OIAF '96 when I observed Frédéric Back shaking his head in disgust at Corky Quakenbush's stop-motion parody, *Ragin' Rudolph* (made for the Fox sketch-comedy series *MADtv*). I had nothing against Back or those old guards (though I found *The Mighty River* to be a real snoozer), but I wanted, I guess, to also celebrate the raw and rough stuff too. Sure, *Ragin' Rudolph* wasn't some technical wonder, but it was well written and funny as hell. Plus, I just couldn't—and I still feel this way—tolerate humourless films. Life is short, life can be unbearable and boring and painful. We need to laugh at it all. It's the only defence we have.

Where was I? Right, Round 3.

So, most festivals (including Ottawa for many years) will make the final list of films and then start constructing the screening order. We do it the opposite way. I start constructing each of the film screenings and only when that's done is the selection process complete.

First I sit, cut up the index cards into smaller pieces, and write the title of every film still in consideration on them. With masking tape at hand, I then start constructing. I always start with the opening film. I try to find something upbeat or funny, something that really gets the audience feeling good and welcome. And then it's from there that it all falls into place. From there, I listen for the follow-up. Yes, listen. I replay the end of the first film, really trying to feel the rhythm, and then I start thinking of films that could follow that—not necessarily the same rhythm, but something...well, I can't explain. It's just instinctual. And it continues like that. I also keep in mind whether a film has a lot of dialogue or none or very little. Watching 10–15 films in a 75-minute period requires a lot of sensory energy from the audience. Talkative films are tough alone, so it's best not to put them back-to-back. So that sometimes also plays a role, but in almost all cases I listen to the ends and beginnings of the works.

Now, anyone who knows me knows of my unwavering love for the indie band Guided by Voices and their main guy, Robert Pollard, who is also a collage artist. In fact, his song and lyric construction are often collages as well. He takes the sequencing of his records very seriously and, in fact, maybe that's when I realized that I was constructing competition screenings in a similar style. He's known, especially in earlier days, for including short, almost demo-sounding pieces in between longer, more produced pieces. All of it got me thinking about albums and their construction. When a new record is approaching, a band teases us with singles, generally more poppy or catchy songs. And so often, when we'd heard the whole record, we'd be surprised that the single actually sounds nothing like the rest of the record.

I approach each competition screening like I am sequencing a record album. Maybe this all sounds precious and arty-farty, but it's not. I don't think about it so much while I'm doing it. It's a very instinctual process, but I think it's important you don't just throw the films out there. You're trying to—not exactly tell a story—but create an experience for the audience. And what seems to surprise—many annoy—some people is that, in the end, I'm not necessarily concerned with picking the so-called best films. In the process of constructing each of these five "records," I'll toss out a film that seemed certain to be in simply because it doesn't fit the rhythms I'm trying to build. Conversely, there are sometimes films marked for Panorama (or that had already been rejected) that make their way back because I found a space where the film works wonderfully. In this sense, it's very much like making a record. Not every song on the album will be a hit; some are included because they just fit well, they feel right, even if they might not be the best songs. And yes, sometimes maybe you see three films from the same country or using similar techniques. Those are things that I just don't care much about.

Maybe that irritates some animators, but this all comes back to what I said earlier: competition is nonsense. And, I mean, if I was just picking films that I truly loved, the competition might last 15–20 minutes! There's always compromise involved. And frankly, the line between competition, Panorama (the out-of-competition "best of the rest" screenings), and "rejection" (I hate that word) is often very slim.

In general, I don't think festival programming/curation gets much acknowledgement or love, though in recent years I have had people approach me to talk about the sequencing, which is really nice. I love hearing that someone notices that there is someone taking time and care to create, hopefully, an interesting screening experience. It's also always interesting when people see threads in a screening that I never considered or noticed. It's funny, sometimes I'll look back at the competition selection from a past OIAF, and I can actually see signposts that reflect what was going on in my life (maybe some parenting issues, addiction or grief, etc.).

I'm not writing all of this to say "oh, I'm doing something so much better than everyone and so unique." Not at all. I found a way, as I've done throughout my life in animation, to make the work adapt to me and my strengths.

Strangely, in the years when we had selection committees, we'd receive some really angry letters, phone calls, and—yes—faxes. They would admonish us for not selecting their "brilliant" work. The odd thing was it was the committee that made the decision, not the OIAF itself. Since we started doing it internally, we don't get criticized as much. That said, I don't receive or see any correspondence related to film decisions. My colleagues know that I might potentially write a reply that won't be received well.

But, yeah, the driving force for me has always been what a film says and why. Of course, how they express it (design, technique) plays some role, but it's secondary to me. Do you have anything interesting to say? Is it genuine, is it urgent? Is it coming from a real place? Just as people always refer to my dislike of Alexander Petrov's *The Old Man and the Sea*, I always use J.J. Villard's student film, *Son of Satan* (based on a Charles Bukowski story), as an example of what floats my boat. It's a crudely drawn film with a distorted soundtrack. It makes *Beavis and Butt-Head* look like Disney. There was just something so raw, so visceral, and powerful about it. It was about a young bully who, we learn, is being abused by his father. You rarely saw topics like this dealt with in animation (and it was a topic that was very close to home for me). It was just so refreshing. So, who cares if it's ugly to look at or if the soundtrack is distorted? It fits this difficult story so perfectly. A beautifully crafted work would not remotely fit the content.

—

Since we're talking about presentation, let me briefly explain two other traditional aspects of the festival that we toyed with.

One we've kept—but changed—is our *Meet the Filmmakers* sessions. This is where the OIAF audience talks with the attending competition filmmakers. In the early years we had guest moderators running those discussions, but over time I felt that was the wrong approach. If I'm the one selecting the films, I should be the one talking to the filmmakers. Otherwise, you get that awkward situation—I've had it at other festivals—where you're interviewing someone about a film you didn't really like. I think it's part of the Artistic Director's job to be the bridge between the filmmakers and the audience. And like with the other on-stage stuff, I've always tried to make it loose and funny so people aren't scared to ask questions. Why should it be so bloody serious?

IMAGE 5.4 Chris takes a call during OIAF15 Meet the Filmmakers

One thing we've gotten rid of almost entirely is those paper-wasting welcome pages from assorted organizers, government officials, and sponsors. The other thing we tossed in the late 1990s was the live versions of those, too. It's standard fare for most festivals to have long, snoozy openings featuring a parade of speakers few people know or care about.

I was always terrified of public speaking. Even playing in bands, I preferred to just play guitar and avoid the mic. When I had to go onstage the first time in 1996 for the OIAF opening, I wore a suit and tie and had a prepared speech littered with the usual clichés ("Welcome, friends old and new…"—a line that still gets trotted out by unimaginative speakers every year). It was awful. I was shaking and reading like a robot. Then we'd have officials—who'd rather be anywhere else—reading words they didn't write about a festival they barely knew. The audience squirmed politely but just wanted the films. It was absurd. Why do we torture ourselves like this? Sure, some festivals say sponsors insist on stage time. Maybe. But there are other ways—logo slides, a quick 30-second video—without putting everyone to sleep.

I think it was OIAF '98, thanks to an interrupting baby in the audience, that I realized we could just get rid of the stiff stuff and have some fun. I started improvising, reacting to the baby, and people laughed (a dangerous drug), and that was that.

IMAGE 5.5 Joel Frenzer, Lei Lei, and Alan Foreman rap at OIAF11

At OIAF '00 we began our tradition of absurdist openings. Inspired by Andy Kaufman, I walked onstage in a neck brace. With me was Korbett Matthews in a doctor's outfit pushing a wheelchair. A Sheridan friend had sent me a book of poems written by a policeman in the 1970s. I read two of them, sat in the wheelchair, and we left. That was the whole opening.

To ease my stage anxiety, I started imagining I was some mix of Buster Keaton and Dean Martin. I stopped using scripts—just the occasional index card. I'd stumble and bumble, and that became the joke. I basically normalized my discomfort.

Other years, I'd stand there saying nothing for five minutes, and I'd planted people in the audience to start heckling me. Another year, I announced the award winners before the competition even started—fake Estonian films, of course (people were calling me the "Estonian guy" then). Another time I found a speech online for a banana festival in Australia and read it almost straight while talking about storms and monkeys and crop failures, and nobody knew what was happening. It got even weirder when four mascot characters kept interrupting me.

In 2010, two animators-turned-podcasters, Joel Frenzer and Alan Foreman, were at the festival interviewing people. I did an interview with them that was so bizarre and fun that afterwards I asked them back to co-host the next year's opening and closing. Instant hit. We even did a talk show format where winners came up and sat on a sofa. When Alan got busy, Joel and I became the duo. We started doing intros for each competition, with Joel appearing as "the Notetaker," secretly drawing onscreen while I was giving announcements, usually making fun of me. It was hard not to look up when the audience was laughing at something I hadn't said.

One year, for *Gertie the Dinosaur*'s anniversary, Annecy did the big, proper version. We did the half-assed one. Joel projected *Gertie* onscreen and did the voice, and I interviewed her.

My all-time favourite gag spanned two festivals. For our 40th, Joel suggested we bring back a hologram of Norman McLaren. Every night we "apologized" for technical difficulties. Of course, we never planned to do it. Then in 2017, Joel actually figured it out with a full-size cutout and projection, and I interviewed McLaren.

As for the festival book greetings: we've mostly ditched them. For a while I wrote fake ones—from made-up people, or surreal haikus (and also using a stranger's face as a stand-in for mine), or me wandering the office and asking staff what they wanted to say. One year we left the lines blank so readers could write their own.

Look, none of this was top-shelf comedy. I just wanted the audience to feel welcome and to understand from the start that we don't have to take this all so seriously. I certainly didn't take all of it seriously. That doesn't mean I don't put my best into everything, but at the end of the day, come on—this isn't a big deal. Yes, we have films and competitions and career stuff, but mostly we're here to be together—to laugh, get teary, drink, dance. Joel made that fun again for me, too. It probably rescued a couple of years where my enthusiasm was fading.

I'm not trying to claim I'm special or that Ottawa invented anything. I just don't think festivals have to cling to every tired, tedious tradition. Think about the audience. Make it human. I'd rather fail trying to do something a bit livelier and sillier than succeed at something utterly dull and cliché. And if some people don't like the onstage stuff—that's fine. My wife doesn't find me funny either. So be it.

IMAGE 5.6 Hologram Norman McLaren at OIAF17

IMAGE 5.7 Joel and Chris onstage at OIAF19

CHAPTER 6

Between Fact and Fiction

Writing Animation

People call me—when they're being polite—an animation critic, journalist, historian, writer. All of those make me squirm. There are people who actually do that work properly: John Canemaker, Giannalberto Bendazzi, Olga Bobrowska, Maureen Furniss, Alla Gadassik. I never set out to be "Animation Guy." I just didn't leave.

And, honestly, this chapter makes me uncomfortable. The whole book does. I said I'd write it, so here we are. But writing, for me, was never "behold my genius"; it was how I educated myself and tried to make sense of the room I walked into. In this case, the room happened to be animation.

Faulkner is supposed to have said, "I don't know what I think until I read what I said." Joan Didion said it cleaner: "I write entirely to find out what I'm thinking."[1] I wrote because I didn't know. I was trying to find a voice, not a present one fully formed. You'll see a pile of examples in this chapter, but not for a second do I think I'm some master stylist. I'm just a hack muddling through, trying to make animation writing a bit less stiff.

I'm not an animation "fanatic." I rarely watch animation in my free time and I almost never read books about animation. I'd rather listen to comedy, read novels, and fall into music. It just happens that for 35 years animation was the ecosystem I was standing in, so that's what I wrote

DOI: 10.1201/9781003633181-7

IMAGE 6.1 Parade of Books

about. If I'd stayed a parking-lot attendant, I'd be writing about parking lots.

What I'm saying is: writing was the way in. It's how I navigated the world—and this peculiar little world of animation.

—

In my Grade 8 yearbook, I wrote about wanting to be a journalist. I read a fair bit from a young age (nothing difficult, mostly books about hockey and detective series like *The Hardy Boys*). I hated high school and was vacant in most classes, but the class that did eventually wake me up was English. In Grade 10, I remember our teacher, David Gamble, who was so enthusiastic about Shakespeare and books in general that you couldn't help but be inspired. But it was in Grade 12 during Ms. Kingsbury's class that I really got hooked. She was an old-school teacher, very conservatively dressed and behaved. I was often at odds with her and more than once got tossed from class. That changed when we were assigned to read *Fifth Business* by Canadian author Robertson Davies. I can't even remember the book now, but it hooked me instantly (much the way Hitchcock's *Rear Window* did years later in Film Studies), and I loved the idea of writing.

Unfortunately, I was terrified to write—crippling doubt left me frozen and unable to put words down. In high school we had an assignment to write something. I just couldn't do it. I came up with a piece about a guy being trapped in a room for no reason (which, I guess, was about the very act of trying to write). I just had no ideas. It happened with music too: I played guitar, but coming up with my own songs was impossible. Anxiety of influence. I felt everything had been done and couldn't break free of the feeling that every chord or word was just plagiarism.

Sheridan College, of all places, was where I started to loosen up when I wrote those absurd stories I mentioned earlier: "The Man Who Would Be Fruit"—about a guy who turns into a tomato—and "Pylon Man," about a guy who puts on a street pylon and thinks he's a superhero. Of course, he was an idiot. There were a couple of other pieces too (like the aforementioned Elvis-impersonator family sitcom pilot). After Sheridan, Ottawa's then-weekly paper, *Metro*, published a couple of the stories. Even though they were just silly pieces (heavily influenced by Monty Python), it was pretty damn exciting to be published. It gave me a bit of confidence that briefly extended to music, where for a year I actually managed to write a whole bunch of songs (thankfully I can't find the recordings anywhere!).

In university, I was forced to write essays for film, literature, and music history classes. I tried so hard to write in that dry, academic tone, but it just wasn't in me. I did my best and got good grades, but it never felt genuine.

The first animation pieces I wrote—on hockey, Raimund Krumme, and George Griffin—for the OIAF programme book and Canada's *FPS Magazine* were straightforward and carried the academic stench.

All of that started to change sometime in the mid/late 1990s. An old professor of mine, William Straw (who we adored because he could take the most difficult theoretical texts and make them digestible and exciting), recommended a biography about the singer/actor Dean Martin. I had no interest in Dean Martin but decided to give the book a read.

Dino: Living High in the Dirty Business of Dreams (1992) was written by an American named Nick Tosches, and once I started reading, I was completely mesmerized. At the time, I was still pretty naive about the writing world. There were moments where Tosches took you into Dean Martin's mind—you'd be reading what Martin was thinking about working with Jerry Lewis, for instance—and I remember wondering, "How could he possibly know this?" Tosches had never interviewed Martin. Then I realized: "Oh, he's fictionalizing it. He's imagining Dean Martin's thoughts." (Yes, I was a bit daft.)

So here I was, reading a book that on the surface was a biography of an Italian-American singer and his Hollywood career, but it was also about Italian-American life, the mechanics of Hollywood, and even its connections to the mafia. It also explored themes of identity (while Dino's persona was one of a cool, wise-cracking drinker, in reality he would often retreat to his hotel room early, drink milk, and watch old Hollywood westerns on television). Tosches thought Dino was like some modern-day Buddha. He described him as a *menefreghista*, an Italian phrase meaning "one who does not give a fuck." Tosches darted back and forth between the profound and the profane; one minute quoting Dante, the next using street language. By the end of the book I realized that Tosches' fusion of fact and fiction took us to a deeper level of understanding, a deeper truth that facts alone could never reach.

This was a mind-blowing moment for me.

From there I devoured everything Tosches had written and sought out writers who influenced him. I learned that he used to be a rock music critic and was friends with this other oddball writer, Richard Meltzer, whose writing was even more unconventional and almost Dada-like. Sometimes described as the first rock music critic, he wrote the first book of rock criticism, *The Aesthetics of Rock* (1970), that applied philosophical thinking to assorted rock and pop songs. Good luck trying to read it. It's so dense that I often think he's messing with the reader.

Almost immediately I started incorporating some of their approaches in my animation writing. I wrote pieces on Priit Parn and Alexander Petrov (yeah, him again) that were a mix of fact, fiction, and utter b.s. I remember writing crazy pieces about René Jodoin and Jan Lenica. Both pieces appear chaotic and improvised, but I'd actually been reading a lot of books about time (in the case of Jodoin) and absurdist writers like Eugène Ionesco and Alfred Jarry. I was trying—and not necessarily succeeding—to approach the filmmakers and their work in a manner that conveyed the essence of their films in a more playful way.

Until I discovered Tosches and Meltzer, I was mentally constipated; their writing unclogged me. Suddenly I felt loose, light, and free to write.

Oh, and I should say that the whole reason I started writing on animation was first and foremost to educate myself. In those days, there were books about every god-damn detail of a Disney, Warners, or Fleischer film, but virtually nothing on animation outside of the U.S., except for a few pieces on Norman McLaren, the Brothers Quay, Jan Švankmajer, and Yuri Norstein. Having suddenly taken over one of the largest animation festivals on the planet, I had to educate myself pretty fast, and the best way to do that was to watch the films, meet the animators, talk with them, interview them, and then write.

I was lucky enough to have an instant outlet via the OIAF catalogues, but soon I started writing for other publications like AWN, *Plateau Magazine*, *ASIFA Magazine* (where I'd take over as editor in 2001), etc.

As I wrote earlier, I first started writing for AWN's *Animation World Magazine* in 1997 when I published a rant about ASIFA-International. Later in 1997, I wrote a piece for them on the Children's Television Workshop and MTV. From there I wrote pieces on Ryan Larkin, Jan Lenica, and Canadian animation.

In October 2001, I wrote a piece that stemmed from my growing frustration with the general atmosphere at festivals. The late 1990s were a wild time in animation. Studios had money, the dot-com boom was brewing, and animation was thriving—feature films, TV series, commercials, music videos. Channels like Teletoon and Cartoon Network were seeking content. Studios were hosting massive parties at festivals—in Annecy, Stuttgart, and Ottawa—trying to scout talent and find new ideas.

Eventually, I began to feel uneasy about all of it. I felt like I was playing the role of a pimp—connecting studios and students who wanted jobs. Both sides wanted something from the other, and I was in the middle, benefitting in some way. In October 2001, I wrote that text under the heading "The Animation Pimp."

Here's that first text in full:

Few years back was planning a piece bout (not boot) festival directors bein' pimps. Johns and hoes are interchangeable (e.g. Joe animator is a John looking for a hand-job from a studio and also a ho offering the studio guy/gal themselves as a whore/john, a tidy, quick piece o meat). The whole shaaaaabang of them (whether Russian animators or California buyers) straddle the line. This was about 96 when festivals became a site of decadence.

Figured festivals were/should be galleries, museums, venues for artists to gather and share ideas, work and experiences. I hate galleries and museums. Damn stagnant receptacles for the glorification of the artist as GREAT (WO) MAN. Needless to say these artsy circle jerks didn't attract the public who don't seem to understand the term animation. Should we use Animation Film Festival anyway? Maybe Cartoon Festival is more public friendly. Yeah...International Cartoon Film Festival. The (point) being that the festivals were elitist.

Then Big Bird convinced Siebert that cartoonies could in fact sell coolness and More Tittie Visuals were born. And so began the wallpapering of animation. Festivals changed. Suits started comin'. Students came to find jobs, not ideas cause ideas don't buy Nikes (i.e. coolness). Studios came to show their human side, headhunt, steal new styles (ya ever notice that Rugrats, Duckman and the whole Csupo look borrows a bit from a well known Estonian animator who influenced the Ukes who were lushingly lured to Hollywood?) and wank. Nuttin wrong with that s'long as they payin'.

Same time governments turned right and figured that cartoons weren't no important ding to be payin' for so might as well let da' mouse cover it. Welcome booths.

Ottawa is not so bad I guess because Annecy has whored itself worse than any of us (Roy Disney! Give me a fuggin' break.). But hell, they attract a shitload of people and studios and sponsors so I guess maybe it's a good thing, but I tell you each year I plan the festival's programme with no freakin idea how much money I will have. So maybe I'm just jealous (then again...Europe has more bodies then Canada).

The Ottawa Festival is a crapshoot. We plan the programmes, hire staff, invite programmers and guests but have no clue if we will make enough money. "Yeah," says Terry American, "but you're government supported up dere in your socialist country." A fallacy. Twenty percent of our budget is covered by the government: $24,000 (City of Ottawa), $90,000 (Telefilm Canada), $15,000 (National Film Board of Canada), $4,500 (Region of Ottawa-Carleton). Considering our size, history and importance in North America these numbers are disgusting.

My demonic inner voice, while dropping the kids at the pool, yells, "IF WE WERE IN TORONTO!" Of course, the funny thing is that we work hard to avoid showing cartoons and try to convince people that animation is an art form. This never works and in the end if we simply resorted to showing funny cartoonies we'd be on our way...media attention would flow in every direction. But then where are we? We've got press but it's for all the big companies who are getting it already anyway...the independents and small companies are left in the dark again.

The media doesn't care about Andreas Hykade, Paul Driessen or Raoul Servais. They are more interested in some Ottawa schmuck who is inkin' dogs for some half-butt TV production.

Intermission

Whining aside, this is an ok job. I make my hours, travel around the world. I write.

Where am I going with this anyway? I think I was more in love with the title and trying to shock people than saying anything relevant or new. This year, Ottawa felt good. We maybe broke even.

Maybe I'm suggesting that the heart and soul of a festival remains in those dark spaces. Don't be fooled by the facades of the suits and the logos. This is just foreplay. The real down and dirty stuff lies within those silent, dark walls which come alive in a sensual play of light and sound that bring pleasure, pain, ecstasy, laughter, insight, shock, guffaws, grunts, groans. Within the shadows these sounds bring you closer to you and those around you. The rest is just whoring. So in the end me and my fellow pimps and pimpettes offer everything for the needy starved festival-goer. If you want quick, no bullshit solo action, we've got booths and rooms for you. If you want more intimate, interactive, in-depth experiences (e.g. group sex?) we've got a nice dark 969 (not shittin ya) seat space for you. And if you just want to talk that's ok too. But no profanity.[2]

Yeah, I was trying too hard, but there was also a genuine attempt to break free of stuffy animation writing and have a bit of fun with it—something I definitely got from Richard Meltzer and, to a lesser degree, Hunter S. Thompson. Soon after, it hit me that this could be a regular column. AWN agreed. Over the next five years or so, I had the best time of my life writing monthly columns. A column needed an image, and during a drinking session with the German animator Andreas Hykade, he roughly drew the first Pimp illustration.

That column unexpectedly launched a whole new chapter for me. Some people were offended by the title—claiming it was sexist or inappropriate—but I never quite understood that, especially since the stereotype of a pimp is usually male. But, boy, were the comments mixed and often hostile. If there was any doubt how conservative and safe this animation community can be, the reactions to the Pimp columns stamped it.

And no, I wasn't always trying to provoke. I was just having fun with adopting different voices (like a sexist, Foucault-quoting rapper), playing with format and structure (writing a text that you had to read from right to left; doing a review of the feature *Jimmy Neutron* that was composed entirely of blank pages), listing various people who also hated *The Old Man and the Sea* (an idea I totally stole from Meltzer):

> This is Pascal Blais' favourite cartoon. It's Bernard Lajoie's 2nd favourite toon. It's Martine Chartrand's 3rd favourite toon. It's Sofi Valliant's 4th favourite toon. It's Alexander Petrov's 5th favourite toon. It's Sayoko Kinoshita's 6th favourite toon. It's Mariel Hemingway's 7th favourite toon. It's Anthony Quinn's 8th favourite toon. It's Gordon Pinsent's 9th favourite toon. It's Normand Roger's 10th favourite toon. It's the guy who runs Annecy's 11th favourite toon. It's the woman/man he's fuggin's 12th favourite toon. It would have been John Denver's 13th favourite toon. It was the woman who did *South Park* but died's 14th favourite toon. It's Leonard Maltin's 15th favourite toon. It's Jean-Guy, my barber's 16th favourite toon. It's Paul Reuben's 17th favourite toon. It's Elizabeth Taylor's 18th favourite toon. It's EVERYONE who's fucked Elizabeth Taylor's 19th favourite toon. It's Tom Knott's 20th favourite toon. It's

> Jacques Parizeau's 21st favourite toon (doesn't like immigrants or women). It's Stumpy Bouchard's 22nd favourite toon ('cause Jack told him so). It's Mr. T's 23rd favourite toon. It's Quebec's 24th favourite toon. It's Patrick Roy's 25th favourite toon. It's the inventor of Kleenex's 26th favourite toon. It's "We're gonna need a bigger boat's," 27th favourite toon. It's June Foray's 28th favourite toon. It's George Jones' 29th favourite toon. It's Nick Tosches' 30th favourite toon. It's the guy who drove Di to her death's 31st favourite toon. It's the old man's 32nd favourite toon. It's Jesus Christ's 33rd favourite toon. It's his friend's 34th favourite toon. It's David Cross' 35th favourite toon. It's the guy he works with's 36th favourite toon. It's my dog's 37th favourite toon. It's "Lola's" 38th favourite toon. It's "Koko's" 39th favourite toon. It's my bitch's (other dog) 40th favourite toon. It's Xena's 41st favourite toon. It's Very Duffy's 42nd favourite toon. It's Michael Caine's 43rd favourite toon. It's Terry Sawchuck's 44th favourite toon. It's Pete Townshend's 45th favourite toon. It's June Christy's 46th favourite toon. It's Hot Tuna's 47th favourite toon. It's Emmet Miller's 48th favourite toon. It's ASIFA's 49th favourite toon. It's ASIFA-Canada's 50th favourite toon ('cause Ocelot told 'em so). It's Kirikou's 51st favourite toon. It's that little Cuban kid's 52nd favourite toon. It's his uncle's 53rd favourite toon. It's his dad's 54th favourite toon. It's the soldier who held the gun's 55th favourite toon. It's some Japanese corporation's 56th favourite toon. It's IMAX's 57th favourite toon. It's my ass' 58th favourite toon. It's Andy Griffith's 59th favourite toon (he was hoping to star). It's Wolverine's 60th favourite toon. It's Laura Dern's 61st favourite toon. It's Deion Sanders' 62nd favourite toon. It's Pinball Clemon's 63rd favourite toon. It's Pinball Wizard's 64th favourite toon. It's some fugger at Disney's 65th favourite toon. It's my mom's 66th favourite toon. It's whomever my dad is' 67th favourite toon. It's Richard Meltzer's 68th favourite toon. It's my 69th favourite toon.[3]

I wrote about trying to get aroused by animation porn films; I took Kant's notions of taste and applied them to animation; I explored Epicurus's thoughts on pleasure in the context of the Aardman series *Rex the Runt*; and I pondered Donald Duck's sanity in a piece called "Donald Duck Is an Asshole."

IMAGE 6.2 The original Animation Pimp logo by Andreas Hykade

In cartoon world, Fred Flintstone wasnt even the first, second or third all-out asshole. Before him there was UPAs Pete Hothead, a man who ran around screaming like a jackass over the slightest set back. Before that there was Daffy Duck and hell even Bugs Bunny. In truth, isnt Bugs more of an asshole than Daffy? Daffy clearly has a neurological disorder and is hardly conscious of his deeds. Bugs, though, is clearly in full possession of his faculties and quite conscious of his evils.

But these folks are farm team material compared to the master ass of them all: Donald Duck. Hes the Gordie Howe of assholes. Seventy years. Thats quite an achievement. Yes sirree. Im 37. Im sure youll agree that Ive had many asshole moments in my life, but Id be hard pressed to say that Ive been an ass or even arse-hole my ENTIRE life. Ive had minutes, hours, days maybe even weeks where Ive been as close to angelic as me or you are likely to get. Donald, though, has been an asshole during EVERY minute moment of his existence. That takes a special type of creature. Not even Donald Trump can match that yet.

> Just before and after viewing entries for Ottawa 04 (which left me in a bit of Donald state), I sat down and watched the latest *Disney Treasures: On the Front Line*, and *Chronological Donald*. Like most Ive always liked Donald. Found him ridiculous and loved seeing him spaz out over every slight setback. However, watching them again without the abstract lenses of youth, I found the character frustrating and tragic.[4]

One of my all-time favourites, "Via Slug's Saloon" (taken from the title of a free-jazz recording by Albert Ayler), was a maddening, unedited, stream-of-consciousness piece that tried to take the reader into every second of the festival selection process. It's almost impossible to read, which was kind of the point. Here's an excerpt from that madness:

> *One will be the more learned, the more one knows that one is ignorant.* – Nicholas of Cusa
>
> Oh my god No phukking way Good story but same ol same ol Ginger can kiss my green grass ass Self-conscious hip Speaking of enemas Technique is unique but this is phukking boring Narration is weird disjointed intense Hey these animals are really cute Pushing the Canadian accents to extremes Fairly Hey a freak dog with three legs Cow cud with big balls Been there seen that Blah blah Bangles Eat me! I would like to sock someone Im feeling violent the clichés never end Disney has redefined bland nice bosom though pro-girl but of course shes ummhot I like tea biscuits I smell monkey poo We are talking about blueberry chocolate confusions sometimes I think its chocolate but its blueberry Nice design Jerry Stiller bird I like blueberry tea biscuits Ive had 2 cups of coffee Disneys answer to Powerpuff Design=Burton Jokes=lame Id rather eat rice Pretty phukking obscure Really a series? Pretty funny Cleaning rooms is a no-go Winking is a no-no One bite of a cabbage and his wish will come true Suck my cakehole ya bad acting bitch Pretty original but I dunno kinda boring too Theres that dog again A fart joke multiple orgasms hand in pants vomiting little hairy muffin Every lame idea becomes a TV concept it's like a phukking receptacle looks like an early '80s cartoon but would look bad even then A meccano dream here we go again first Elvis reference Belongs in heaven lame jokes poor dialogue Nathan Lane!? Ive had better tales in my ass Cereal company doesnt

but toys in box Igors character influence Not on tape Blow me! Annecy can keep it! Decent design mediocre script Pre Dickable Holy phuk. See "mimi"

Now THATs animation! This music is making me thirsty No way Nice Mexican accent ya skinny phuck is a dog aware of his existence? Dont be greedy come and get it no its wrong here try some ge ya goin real big fat albert

#1

my nose runs on occasion there is a no in nose I am a no

I hate elves and for dummie books die please light green has that overbeck look red while circle dancers in circle I was nice ONCE not again Stay there youre more boring than your boring city Ruined by coupling duck hunt Theyre shooting ducks slike a fortune tellereh HA HA HA Reindeers drinking stupid old broad Sometimes when I crap it 's poignant Phuck U That rough raw style Fresh towels are fine Flutes should be banned Elastic band MAYBE just because there are three people and I am but one who said NON! Make the pain go away Great gag Bugs can't play drums 9–11 reference #1 How come the Penguin? I wanna work for Don Bluth, but Don Bluth doesnt work anymore either Hes phukkin dreamin in pencil Heyfran/will Krause influenced! Thick line drawings slavery bit of Larkin influence Elderly schmelderly RRRRRRRRRRRR Why is this animated? So much realistic detail Just shoot it LIVE! Maybe Can. Panorama It's NEVER Jules Verne? Character design is just silly Clitoris? It belongs in a hole St. inspector Nein This is one of the WORST entries ever cheese burger amiga man I feel like sleeping too A lo ghostbuster with a halo/belly button De la A La Nice bits poor pace at times not always clear something familiar Woody Allen Big eyed guy in cub sketchy style even worse then the Quays Nails cotton and things that dont move Great voice actors! I was out-voted so its maybe for panorama Frankenstein created turns on creator? Im losing my mind on Day 2 I dont like my mummy bunny honey huuney strange atmospheric not THAT bad woman as oven max schrek that damn 2d look heythat guy has no nose but he does have a trailer Oh dear now hes a bird Why? The new King! Softfocus Nobut I do! Preachy but nice design so-so so-so mmmmmhp sauce [I made a drawing too] I dont like red landscape First we drink[5]

And yes, in all those pieces, the grammar and spelling "mistakes" were intentional. Another thing I did a lot—and still do—was attribute real quotes to the wrong person. One example:

> *This philosophy recognizes as the true thing, not the thing as it is an object of the abstract reason, but as it is an object of the real, complete man.* Deion Sanders, The Essence of Primetime.[6]

The quote was actually from *The Essence of Christianity* by Ludwig Feuerbach, but I always got a kick out of taking these weighty quotes and assigning them to the most unlikely sources—in this case, the former football and baseball player Deion "Primetime" Sanders.

Was it occasionally pretentious and juvenile? Yep. No doubt. And there are definitely pieces that make me cringe, but I worked hard on them, and I've never had more fun writing than I did then. When we compiled the best columns into the book *The Animation Pimp* (2007), I had to revisit everything, and I could clearly see that—aside from the influence of Tosches and especially Meltzer, with maybe a bit of Hunter S. Thompson (though I hadn't really read him until later) and the Beat/New Journalism people—my Film Studies background was all over the pieces. I was revisiting Michel Foucault, Roland Barthes, Pierre Bourdieu, and other thinkers I'd first encountered in Will Straw's classes.

After I retired the column in 2005, it was suggested we take the best of them and turn it into a book. Andreas Hykade agreed to do illustrations for each column. His work—and our shared love of dumb humour and old rock, blues, and folk—added another layer to the texts. Each drawing was its own thing and totally him.

Like I said, there was a lot of hostility towards me in those days. You can still find most of the comments. For a highly sensitive person, it was a jolt. This was early internet—people could react to you almost instantly. Sometimes I took it too personally and fired back too fast, but over time it taught me to chill out and stop letting every random opinion through the armour. So when we needed back-cover blurbs, I figured the best way to defuse the critics was to use them—grab the harshest (printable) comments and stick them on the book.

Before the *Pimp* book, I'd already published a few other books—two of them on hockey. One was a light, kid-meets-nostalgia kind of thing, like the hockey books I grew up on. The other, *Stole This From a Hockey Card*, was much more personal—very Dino-inspired—not only about the

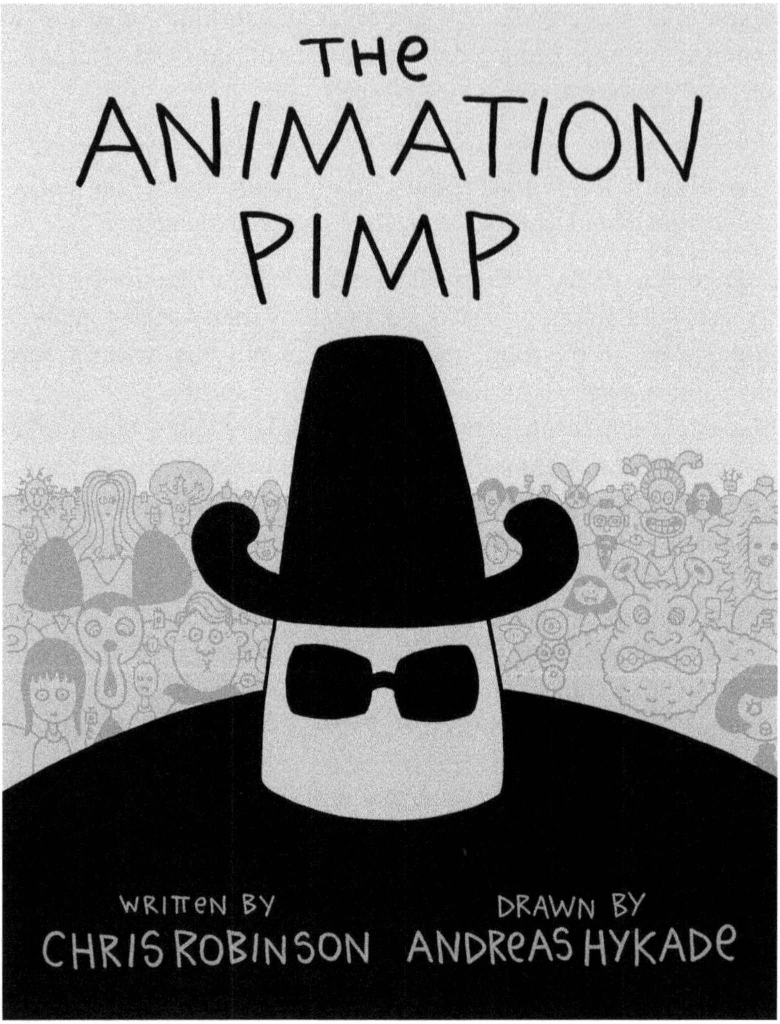

IMAGE 6.3 Early version of *The Animation Pimp* book cover

star hockey player, Doug Harvey, but also about my childhood, identity, and addiction. That one was my first semi-success: award nominations, invites to writers' festivals, and a glowing review in *The Globe and Mail* (our Canadian *NYT Book Review*).

I'd also written two animation books: *Estonian Animation: Between Genius and Utter Illiteracy*, a history of the Estonian scene I fell in love with, and *Unsung Heroes of Animation*, a collection of texts about independent animators that still seems to resonate.

IMAGE 6.4 *The Animation Pimp* book reading and exhibition at OIAF07

When the *Pimp* book was almost ready, we figured it should have a foreword. Since Richard Meltzer—who I'd already met and traded emails with—had given me a blurb for *Stole This From a Hockey Card*, I didn't want to hit him up again. So I took a swing at Nick Tosches (who was pretty well known by then). An animation acquaintance, Deb Dawson, was a Tosches fan and somehow had his mailing address. She passed it on. I wrote him, sent the cover of *Unsung Heroes of Animation*—which was a straight homage to his *Unsung Heroes of Rock and Roll*, doing for animators what he'd done for overlooked musicians—and asked if he'd write a back-cover blurb.

I don't remember the exact date—probably Christmas 2006. My friend Barry was over with his wife and daughter. That was also the night our son Jarvis split his chin on the corner of our table, so we spent the evening at the hospital. In the middle of all that, an email arrived from Nick Tosches. He said he was glad I'd written and that he'd do it—not just a blurb, but an introduction to *The Animation Pimp*. I was floored. We even talked about me coming to New York.

Yeah, I was in heaven.

Even better was his eventual text:

> Writers who don't, so to speak, pull off their britches when they write don't write anything worth reading. It is good, in a pathetic sort of way, that writers do, so to speak, pull off their britches when they write. Otherwise, there would be far too much to read, and life is far too short.
>
> But Chris Robinson's writing should be read. His honesty, what he has to say, and how he says it are enthralling. This is the real thing by a real writer.
>
> It's uncanny, very uncanny, that if you're looking for writing about animation, you'll find it here, and if, like me, you're not, you won't. I don't quite know how this can be, but it is.

It's that last passage that got me. It was about animation and yet not at all about animation.

Maybe part of why I was disenchanted with the OIAF during those years was because I was writing more—and writing about subjects outside animation. Plus, Kelly and I had our second son, Harrison, around then, so life was getting crazier and the festival appealed to me less and less.

I even foolishly believed that the critical success of *Stole This From a Hockey Card* (which, you animators should know, was rejected by 10–15 publishers before it found a home) would launch me into a literary career.

Ha ha ha, silly me.

After *The Animation Pimp*, I wrote *Canadian Animation: Looking for a Place to Happen* (2008), a strange travelogue triggered by a job I got from the Canadian government. They asked me to write a report on the state of the Canadian animation industry. My job was to fly across Canada meeting and interviewing studios and industry people. I figured, hell, why not casually interview all these independent animators spread out across the country too. Then came *Ballad of a Thin Man: In Search of Ryan Larkin* (2008), which I've already mentioned. It was a strange book—part biography, part personal book about fathers, Bob Dylan, and the people we put on pedestals—and then *Animators Unearthed* (2010), a more conservative sequel to *Unsung Heroes of Animation*.

Later in 2010 I published *Japanese Animation: Time Out of Mind*. Alongside *The Animation Pimp* and *Stole This From a Hockey Card*, this might be my favourite book. It's not perfect, but it's one of the few times I basically achieved—however flawed—what I set out to do.

IMAGE 6.5 Unsung Heroes of Animation

That book was born out of guilt. I'd received this incredible grant from the Japan Foundation. They'd fly me first class to Japan for two weeks, give me an escort (no, not that kind) and an interpreter, and let me do whatever I wanted. It was an insanely generous offer. But I felt guilty, so I thought I should do something work-related while I was there. I contacted my main animation publisher, John Libbey, and proposed writing a book on independent Japanese animators. He agreed, and suddenly my schedule was filled with interviews in between visits to Kyoto, Hiroshima, and sumo matches.

It was my first time in Japan, and Tokyo immediately overwhelmed me. It felt like standing where past, present, and future all cross. When I got home, I started diving into Japanese films and books, but two other things pushed the book in a different direction. As I said before, my oldest friend, Barry, dropped dead in 2009 while I was writing. I struggled hard with his death. I lost my footing and went into an almost comatose depression. The other influence—way less dramatic and much sillier—was finding (probably on YouTube) a special called *Big Bird in Japan*. In this goofy show, Big Bird goes to Japan, loses his host, and just wanders around meeting people.

Boom—there it was. In that haze of grief and disorientation, I'd be the lost protagonist in Japan, wandering around and "just happening" to meet all these odd, brilliant people who happened to be animators. And that's what I did. It's not an easy book if you don't know the films or filmmakers, but I was trying to dodge the usual "here's their bio and filmography" model. I wanted something sparse that carried the tone of each animator's work, something you could feel. And in a country that's given us Godzilla and Murakami, a non-linear, slightly off-kilter book felt right.

Another influence that slipped into the mix was Bob Dylan. I'd never been a big Dylan admirer until he released a run of records that really hit me: *Time Out of Mind* (1997), *Love and Theft* (2001), *Modern Times* (2006), and *Together Through Life* (2009). Around then there was also a little controversy about *Love and Theft* and a Japanese book, *Confessions of a Yakuza* (1989), by Junichi Saga—people accused Dylan of lifting a few text fragments. It was never really settled. Saga didn't make a fuss and actually said that if Dylan was influenced, he was honoured.

So just for once, I thought I'd seek revenge for Japan. Throughout the book I quietly dropped in random Dylan snippets into what I titled *Time Out of Mind*.

Here's an excerpt from the book just to show the novel-ish tone of it. The underlined bit (in the original) nods to two Dylan songs:

> Pissing down snow today. Apparently it's a cold winter here. I find it warm.
>
> I'm walking through the streets feeling a million miles from home.
>
> A deep booming voice interrupts my thoughts: "Chris Robinson".

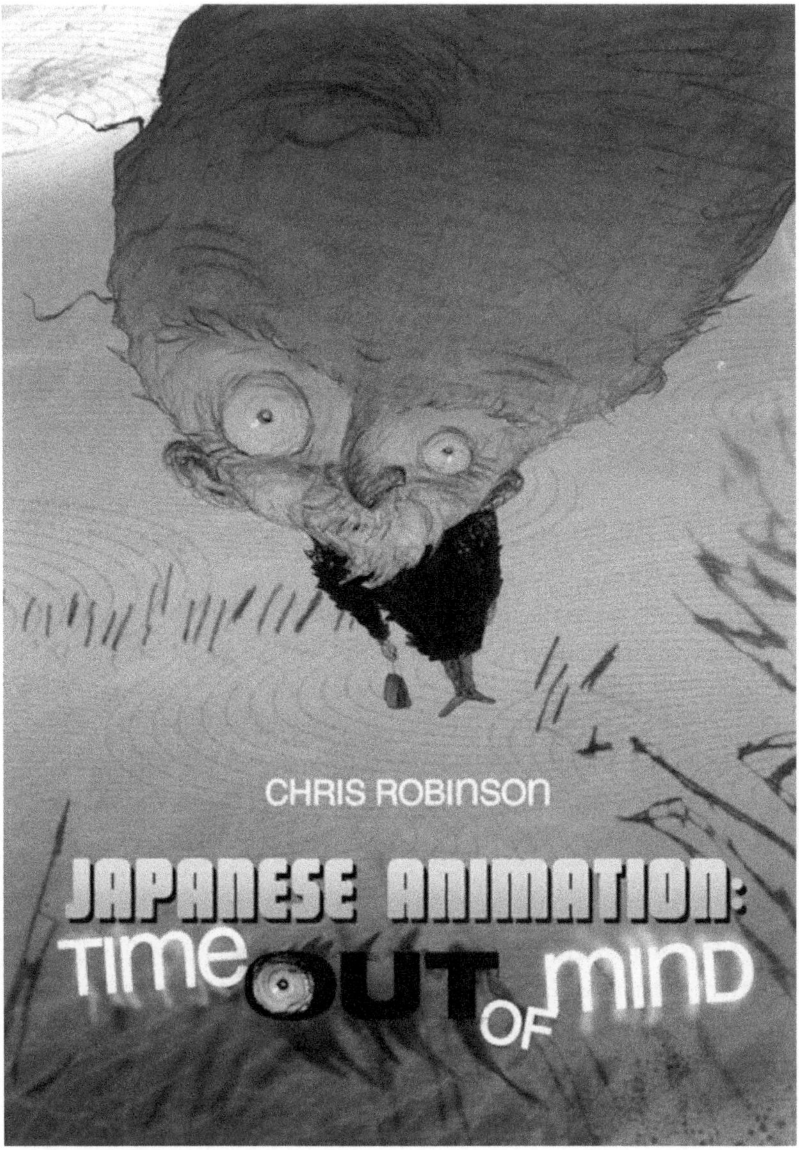

IMAGE 6.6 Time Out of Mind

I look around and just see people hurrying nowhere fast. I keep walking.

"CHRIS ROBINSON!"

I stop, look around again. Nothing.

"LOOK TO THE SKIES!"

I stop and look up and see a face inside a large grey cloud.

"I AM NAOYUKI TSUJI!"

I scratch my head and say nothing.

"YOU MUST TELL THEM ABOUT ME."

"Tell who what?"

"THE PEOPLE OUT THERE WATCHING US."

"Are you nuts? There's no one watching us. Do you see people out there watching us?"

"I SEE ALL. I SEE THE ENTIRE PICTURE. THEY ARE OUT THERE IN HOMES, PLANES, TRAINS, BUSES, SUBWAYS, TOILETS, READING THESE WORDS."

This guy's nuts, but I'm not about to argue with a giant face in a grey cloud. So, let me

tell you about Naoyuki Tsuji.

Who is Naoyuki Tsuji? I dunno. Never heard of him before. Guess he doesn't do animation festivals. Where was he born? Does it matter? Do you want to know? I can find out. Hold on …

Someone I don't know says it's 1972. I'll take his word for it. Make "you" feel better?

Oh, he's Japanese. I bet you guessed that already, though.

Does this tell you enough? Do you feel you know him better?

Do you wonder if he's tall or short, thin or fat? What's his favorite colour, favourite song? Where does he live? Is there more than one guy in the world with his name? Does he eat cheese? Can he dance? Does he have legs (one of his characters has no arms)? Can he drive? Did he make me cry once?

Does it matter? Will those things help you know Tsuji any better? Is there a self we can even know? David Hume said that self was nothing but a bundle of different perceptions. So identity depends on which given perception is on stage. I know enough to say that for me Naoyuki Tsuji is the author of *Wake Up* (1992) and *A Feather Stare in the Dark* (2003). However, I can't say that the same Naoyuki Tsuji made these films. Get my drift?

So, yeah, I was experimenting. Did I succeed? No idea. Don't really care, actually. I managed to do what I set out to do. Simple as that.

After a long period of not writing much about animation—at least in book form—I got motivated again during the pandemic, and despite promising myself that each new book would be the last, I somehow kept getting dragged into doing more.

Aside from Hykade (who would later illustrate my magic-realist memoir, *My Balls Are Killing Me*), the other animator who became a frequent collaborator was Theodore Ushev. We'd first met in the early 2000s when he wrote to me about the *Animation Pimp* columns. Later, he illustrated the *Ballad of a Thin Man* book.

During all the icky business about Ryan Larkin, I'd shared an email I'd received in 2004 from a woman (I won't go into details) who briefly mentioned that Larkin was no artistic genius and that a real genius was Arthur Lipsett (he'd been an experimental filmmaker at the NFB; his work inspired George Lucas and Stanley Kubrick).

A couple of years later, around 2006, Theo wrote to me all excited. He'd been looking up this Lipsett fellow and learned that he was living in the same apartment building Lipsett once occupied. He wanted to make a film about Lipsett and wanted me to write the script. I'd never written a script before, but of course I agreed—why wouldn't I give it a try?

I struggled with it for a while, but then thought about the way Lipsett made films. He used found film and audio (often from the NFB's garbage bins). Then, like a collage artist, he cut and pasted images and dialogue to fit whatever theme he was working on. So I thought, ha—then I should get his scripts and do the same thing: cut and paste assorted texts that felt right for telling his story. The end result was an experimental biography—in the spirit of Tosches, actually—that wove in parts of Lipsett's archives and films, my life, my grandmother's home movies, and assorted clips from Keaton, Fellini, and Godard. The end result—beautifully brought to life and structured by Theo—was *Lipsett Diaries*, a work of fact, fiction, memoir, and personal archive.

In 2011/2012, we tried another project—tentatively called *Kitchen Confidential*, about cooking and murder—but it didn't work out. In 2025, my script *Idling* (very loosely inspired by a 1990 summer job in a parking lot) went into production as a live-action feature directed by Theo.

I've gotta say, it's been so damn amazing to have Hykade and Ushev as friends and as visual interpreters and collaborators. It definitely strengthened my words.

—

So, yeah—enough. You get the idea. I didn't start writing about animation because I thought I was the person to do it; I started because I didn't know enough and writing was the only way I could make sense of what

IMAGE 6.7 Chris Robinson and Theodore Ushev during Lipsett Diaries screenings, 2010

I was seeing. I never aimed to be the Grand Poobah of Animation Letters. I'm not. I'm fine, I work hard, and I like messing with the form a bit so it isn't all museum air.

If the books and columns filled a gap for some people, that makes me happy—mostly because it means there were other people out there who also wanted animation writing that could breathe, joke, and wander. That was always the point: treat animation seriously without acting serious.

In the end I was just writing to figure things out—films, festivals, the weird little community around them, and whatever was rattling around in my own head. Everything else—awards, praise, whatever—is gravy and possibly a clerical error.

NOTES

1 Joan Didion, "Why I Write," in *Let Me Tell You What I Mean* (New York: Alfred A. Knopf, 2021), p. 45.
2 https://www.awn.com/blog/animation-pimp-0

3 https://www.awn.com/blog/animation-pimp-old-man-and-sea-plagiarism-not-film
4 https://www.awn.com/blog/animation-pimp-donald-duck-asshole
5 https://www.awn.com/animationworld/animation-pimp-slugs-saloon
6 https://www.awn.com/blog/animation-pimp-donald-duck-asshole

CHAPTER 7

What's Different When Everything Is the Same?

As you might have figured out by now, I'm not a calm or measured person, yet, strangely, when I see new technological changes happening in animation, I find that instead of instantly reacting to something we haven't even begun to comprehend, I try to peek through the door of history.

There are valid concerns about artificial intelligence (AI) destroying jobs and creativity in animation. The snarky part of me looks at the steady stream of human-created drivel that comes out of studios on the industry side and thinks AI might actually be an improvement—it certainly can't be much worse than the uninspired, repetitive garbage we too often see in cinemas and on streaming channels today. Most of that stuff already feels like it was spit out by a robot.

And maybe it's a wake-up call to those who go to schools solely to be trained as animators. That's always mystified me. I've always found it a bit dangerous that schools cozy up to the needs of studios. Studio workflows can change in an instant. New technologies keep emerging. You learn one programme only for it to be out of date tomorrow. Then what? Students and schools should maybe learn the fundamentals of art and artistic expression—get some kind of basic foundation that lessens the shock of change later.

Every new wave forces us to ask whether our training prepared us for change—or just for yesterday's tools. Hell, do artists even need schools?

DOI: 10.1201/9781003633181-8

IMAGE 7.1 Chris Clones at OIAF04

I've never really bought into that whole "you need to know the rules in order to break them." Why? We act like these are gospels, God-given guidelines. We made all this stuff up, gang. We made the rules. We can break them. We can ignore them. I've thought over and over how cinema itself was seen as a threat… how photography was a threat… how "talkies" were a threat. Even books (more specifically the printing press) were seen as a threat to memory and oral storytelling. This is life. All these things come and go—twisting, turning, transforming.

AI should be a gift, like the internet was supposed to be—a big messy public playground. Instead, it's fallen into the fists of power-hungry, profit-drunk maniacs who've bent it into a control panel: segment us, rile us, sell us, pacify us. The tech isn't the rot—the owners, and their incentives, are. So use the tool, sure—but keep your hands on the wheel. Don't let it drive the work—or you.

I think AI can be used as a useful artistic support tool that can function in a way not unlike collage (collage, by definition, consists of found materials created or manufactured by someone else). Even collage techniques have changed. The days of scissors and glue have been replaced for many artists by digital technologies. You can cut and paste with a computer mouse. Sure, it's altered the work, but has it ruined it? Has it destroyed collage? Not at all. It's just different.

—

And it isn't just animators. We don't take courses in how to be a festival programmer or organizer. There's no textbook for pacing a programme,balancing tone, or navigating politics, sponsors, and audiences. You learn by watching thousands of films, getting it wrong in public, listening, arguing, revising. The curriculum is failure + repetition + taste. It's an apprenticeship by exposure. Foundations help, but the job is mostly judgement made on the run.

—

I also remember that around the end of the 20th century many old-school animators frowned upon computer animation. They felt it was destroying creativity, that is the computer would ensure the death of hand-drawn animation and take jobs away. Yet hand-drawn—and handmade—animation continues to be made every day. Maybe some jobs were lost, but new jobs were created. Again, animation wasn't destroyed; it transformed.

During my time, I've seen endless ups and downs in the community. It's not always pleasant. As a festival, we have periods when the industry is suffering and doesn't support festivals. The OIAF is fortunate that we don't put all our eggs in the industry basket and, for now, have decent support from three levels of government in Canada. There were years when government support declined but industry rose a bit. There were times when both were down. It's not fun, of course, but you adjust and do your best to continue—if you want to carry on.

I'm not writing any of this from a place of great knowledge. It's just instinct based on what I've seen over the decades. I really don't have answers, but neither do you. All I know is that in 1992 we had about 750 submissions over a two-year period, and in 2025 we had 2,800 something entries in a one-year period. And that's not even close to revealing just how many films are being created in studios, homes, and basements. Today, there's a whole subculture of animators who make films solely for an online audience. So it seems to me that animation, for the most part, is doing just fine. If people are passionate and devoted to the art form, they'll find a way to make it and get it out into the world. There's a traditional belief that you need studios, or series, or to submit to festivals, etc., but it's not true. That's the way the road has been paved, but that doesn't mean there aren't other roads.

—

I do find it amusing to hear younger animators complaining about funding or about how long it takes to make a film. Most of these voices were born in the digital era. They have no inkling how much more expensive and time-consuming it was to make films by hand or in analog times (an easy comparison might be my mixtape analogy from earlier: today, you can make a playlist of almost any song or artist in seconds or minutes. When we made mixtapes—new and cool for us in the 1980s—you had to sit there and listen to every song play before you went to the next one. It took hours and hours).

All I'm saying is that we need to not only keep an eye open but also take a deep breath. I don't mean be passive—no, be awake, be present—but don't overreact. Don't be a John Woo. Open the door gently, look around the room, and ask questions. Listen, process, and take time before making pronouncements.

I used to read newspaper stories going on and on about the death of handmade animation, but it was nonsense. Every year at the OIAF I continue to see all manner of techniques. The media, of course, loves to bust down the door and react. That's their nature. They don't take time to contemplate. We live in a world that actively discourages contemplation, that wants to keep us distracted, to keep us moving without thinking—forgetting is the goal, it seems. We need to remember; that's how we can make informed decisions going forward.

—

Something that has changed a lot—and that's inevitable given the increased number of films being created—is the content. In the 1990s and before, you didn't often see films being overly personal or dealing with addiction, abuse, mental health, neurodiversity, sexuality, identity, etc. Today, that's changed dramatically. Naturally, that reflects a society that has become more openly engaged in discussing these previously taboo or hush-hush topics. Animators feel more comfortable discussing personal pains. I'd say I started noticing this transition in the early 2000s. However, as also happens during these transitional periods, the pendulum often goes too far the other way. Today, every second film seems to be about some personal ailment. It's frankly gotten a bit tedious and self-indulgent.

This feeling started triggering memories for me of works like Phil Mulloy's. His films were vicious, punk screams at the assorted systems (religion, family, pop culture, government, capitalism) that often destroy people's lives, forcing them into poor choices, or choices between bad and worse. In recent years, I've missed his voice. And I think what people need to wake up to is that depression, anxiety, OCD, addiction, and abuse are often created not by a mucked-up brain or bad parents but by a capitalist system that pits us all against each other and that pushes us into this race to be the best. All these pressures. How can it not destroy you? We are being squeezed and twisted and forced into a system that is not one that fits us naturally. So of course it screws us up and we drink and we smoke and beat loved ones up. We steal and beg and lie. It's so strange that during this time when mindfulness, compassion, and empathy are pushed on us every day through schools, apps, podcasts, etc., we're in a world that is more divided and intolerant than it's ever been. We're pitted against each other by those in power, those who seek to control us. We're distracted and told to blame "others": people who have different languages, colours, or sexual identities than "us." It's a lie. Immigrants and transgender people are not hurting you; the oligarchs, those controlling the system—they're the ones we should be focused on. But until we come together and face that reality, nothing will change. I say this not as some wise old man; it's just logic. I say this because I feel animators need to open the door, the window, and start thinking about this outside world—these systems that are making us sick. If you want to understand your anxiety or whatever ailment affects you, that's where you'll find the answers.

—

Alongside this shift in subject matter, form has stretched too.

In recent years, the landscape of short animation has shifted. More shorts are stretching past the 20-minute mark; some are even nudging up against the unofficial 30-minute limit many festivals subscribe to. (For context: in one recent awards season, three of the five Oscar-nominated shorts were 19 minutes or longer.) You can read this as filmmakers responding to audience appetites or simply as artists pushing into stories that need more time.

Breaking the old-time box lets creators dig into denser narratives and fuller characters, which seems to resonate with modern viewers. Recent long-shorts like Tomek Popakul's *Acid Rain* and *Zima*, Daria Kashcheeva's *Electra*, and Kaspar Jancis's *Antipolis* all challenge the old norm that "over 20 minutes" should be rare and reserved for the exceptional. Even veterans Priit and Olga Pärn wandered into the mid-length zone with their awkwardly timed 32-minute *Luna Rossa*.

"So what?" you might ask. One big consequence: fewer films fit into festival competitions. At OIAF, the selected shorts count has trended down partly because long shorts eat up more running time. In 2014 we showcased 84 shorts; from 2015 onwards that range was roughly 56–68; in 2023—when *Electra*, *Zima*, and *Antipolis* were in the mix—we hit a record-low 40. Long films mean fewer programming slots to spread around.

And no, you can't simply add more screenings. Festivals run on tight schedules, limited venues, and real budgets. When a programme lengthens, something else gives—often variety. That means fewer voices and styles on screen.

On the upside, long shorts let filmmakers practise extended pacing, structure, and character work without the full freight of a feature.

Still, the practical friction is real. Longer shorts can be artistically satisfying, but they create headaches for producers, distributors, and festivals trying to balance run times, attention spans, and costs.

So, where does that leave us? The rise of long shorts exposes a basic tension between creative ambition and practical constraints. Festivals, educators, and distributors will likely need to collaborate more, refine programming strategies and maybe formalize a mid-length category so expectations are clearer. If we can hold space for ambition while protecting breadth, we might even nudge the form forward—toward shorts that manage both depth and economy.

Ambition isn't the enemy; misaligned incentives are. Nowhere shows that more than awards season.

—

The OIAF has been an Oscar-qualifying festival for as long as I've been involved. I don't personally put much stock in the Oscars; to me, it's a largely self-congratulatory industry show. Winning at Annecy, Ottawa, or most animation festivals is often tougher than getting into the Oscar pool. That pool is smaller—nowhere near the 2,500+ shorts the festivals like Annecy or Ottawa receive.

Do I understand why filmmakers chase it? Of course. A nomination can mean exposure, career momentum, and more screenings. No quarrel there. What worries me is how festivals (and sometimes studios) let the Oscar chase distort priorities. Everywhere you look, someone's boasting "Oscar qualifying!"—as if that's the point. Celebrate your awards and identity first; don't outsource your value to someone else's show.

Independent-minded outfits—Miyu, the NFB, and others—do vital work for artists. My concern isn't with the quality of their films; it's with the gravity of awards campaigning. When significant time and budget lean toward a single goal—an Oscar push—there's an opportunity cost: fewer resources for riskier voices, regional outreach, or long-term artist development. For a taxpayer-funded institution, that balance matters even more. Historically, the NFB stood for experimentation, shorts, documentaries, and cultivating Canadian artists for Canadian audiences. I'd love to see that centre of gravity remains there—first and foremost—while still enjoying any international laurels that come along.

So yes: congrats if you get shortlisted or nominated. Just don't let the pursuit of one statuette eclipse the wider ecosystem that actually grows the art form.

—

Another thing that's come out of animation's industry "success" is a certain polish. I can't pull a spreadsheet to prove it, but with the rise of initiatives like CEE Animation (the Central & Eastern European support network that helps with pitching and development), I'm seeing more projects smoothed in similar ways. The idea—guidance on pitches, feedback to refine a project—isn't bad. I get it. But I can't shake the feeling that it's sanding off some of the the edge of being an independent artist.

It starts to creep toward an industry mindset applied to personal work: independent shorts treated like products. You're making a film because you have to say something—because it needs out. I don't love the expectation that animators must pitch performatively to get funding. Show your project, sure—boards, animatic, script, intent. But the whole show-and-dance? That's where it starts feeling off.

Independent animators are nudged into becoming salespeople—performers on cue. That live-action, corporate pitch culture is seeping into short-form animation. Pull it back a bit. Let people make their own work. Let them make mistakes. Let films be not perfect. The result is richer.

—

I know I can sound harsh. Part of it's dry humour; part of it is the reality that festival artistic directors see the whole landscape. We watch almost everything. Patterns pop—recurring themes, familiar design trends, fashionable techniques. What feels singular in your studio often echoes across dozens of other films. None of this is to discourage originality. It's tough love from volume: craft isn't the finish line. What you're saying—and why—matters just as much.

Which brings me to something that bugged me in the 1990s and feels even more present now: we're often too damn nice. Not "kind"—non-critical. We default to surface reactions ("I loved your film") and stop there, especially when the design dazzles or the technique is flashy while the story or idea gets a pass. I'm wary when someone praises my writing or programming without substance. I actually value people who push back—once I get over the sting—so long as it's more than "you suck." That's when a real conversation starts. I tried to make space for that with my *Animation Pimp* columns (they may yet return), but we need more venues for sharp, constructive critique that isn't mean and isn't mush.

I get that it's hard. I've had rejection. I didn't like it. But I'm also my own toughest critic. I can look back at past writing or programming and wince—good. That's growth. If all we trade are compliments, we will stagnate, wilt, and die.

—

I keep saying it: animators should be honest. Programmers too. Too many choices are driven by the name, the trend, the laurels. Unless I'm writing an Annecy preview for AWN or Cartoon Brew, I don't check other festivals' lineups. Laurels don't move me—Berlinale, Cannes, whatever. That's not a dig at those events; it's just not how I programme. I want to respond to what's in front of us. Yes, I jury now and then, so I see what's out there. But I wish festivals were truer to themselves—choose the films that knock them sideways, not the ones they assume audiences or sponsors will bless.

—

And while we're on that topic of selections, can we stop with this naive, hippie nonsense that festivals or art spaces should be safe spaces void of politics? What a load of nonsense. This has maybe been a more prevalent issue since Russia's full-scale invasion of Ukraine in 2022 and the Israel/Palestine conflict. There are some who feel festivals should shut the outside world out. How is that possible? How is that remotely responsible? The animation world does not exist in a bubble. We need to keep the windows and doors open and let the breeze, the storms, the sun in—all of it, the good, bad, and evil. Animation films and festivals should be mirroring society, no matter how fractured and chaotic it might be.

I struggle with this: when a government is actively harming civilians, does showing its artists—some funded, some not—become a kind of laundering? Or is silencing those artists another harm, especially when many oppose their state or have fled it? The slope is slippery: if we start there, where do we stop—because no country is innocent. I don't pretend to resolve it here. For now, I sit with the discomfort, weigh context case by case, and accept that any choice leaves a bruise. Living in Ukraine through large chunks of 2024 and 2025 has only complicated this for me; proximity changes what abstractions feel like.

—

It's inspiring to see how many animation festivals have sprung up and thrived over the last 30 years. I've been damn fortunate to visit many of them, and for me, it's the smaller, DIY festivals that are really special. If I had any advice for programmers, organizers, filmmakers, and students: go to as many festivals as you can. Yes, go to Annecy, Zagreb, and Ottawa and also check out the younger and smaller festivals. I love smaller festivals because you can have more meaningful conversations with people. You're not racing around like you do at Ottawa and especially Annecy. It's more low-key, and I appreciate that.

In 2013, I fell in love with the Animateka Festival in Ljubljana. I loved the atmosphere and team so much that I somehow found myself on staff, working as a programming consultant and co-host of filmmaker talks. The intimacy, humour, and passion of that team helped me—new blood, new energy, different perspectives. In 2018, I think I was officially invited to join the team. I loved it then and still do. It not only let me experience a festival differently, but it definitely injected new enthusiasm and ideas into my work with the OIAF.

An ex-partner didn't think it was a good idea that I was "cheating" on the OIAF and having programming influence at another festival, but I never agreed with that or even understood. First, my OIAF colleagues don't care—it doesn't affect them in any way. Second, my job there is to look at a short list of films (basically the equivalent of the third round of the OIAF), watch them, and give feedback.

I also help sequence the competitions. But I do not have—and don't want—final say in what's chosen. I give my opinion and that's that. What I also love is that Animateka's competition is limited to countries from Central, Eastern, and Southern Europe, so I'm often watching films that maybe didn't make the cut at the OIAF but that I can see have real qualities.

With the filmmaker talks, I co-host with the festival director, Igor Prassel, and I think I've brought a bit of OIAF humour to those sessions. Igor can be intense and very focused on production details; I'm generally lighter and more interested in the content (he's called me "the psychologist"). Altogether, it gives me a valuable look at how another festival runs, and it's nice to contribute and feel useful—and then, at the end of the day, it's not my festival.

And make sure you visit Animafest Cyprus and Anibar (Kosovo). These two festivals share a similar spirit and are unlike almost any other (except maybe the unique New Chitose Airport Animation Festival that, yes, takes place entirely in an airport!). While most animation festivals primarily attract people working in animation, Cyprus and Anibar draw a larger general audience. They run outdoor screenings at night, followed by music. In Cyprus, people travel across the island and even set up tents for the weekend. It's a unique mix of animators and locals. This is essential—and still lacking at almost every animation festival.

Make no mistake: festivals remain vital—even though films are online and more accessible than ever, festivals are still the best place to find quirky, off-the-main-road animation. But too often we're preaching to the converted. That's why it's so refreshing—and hopeful—to encounter festivals that reach beyond the walls of animation and into the larger world.

—

Trivial Pit Stop: Stop treating celebrity auteurs—Miyazaki, del Toro, whomever—as untouchable oracles. Enjoy the work, sure, but don't let hero worship narrow your field of view, especially from artists who know nothing about the festivals or the indie animation community. Festivals have been showing mature, diverse, boundary-pushing animation for decades. Go find it.

—

As broken as this world appears to be right now, when I'm at festivals, sitting next to all manner of diversity, it's really encouraging. When we put down our phones, stop doomscrolling (which is what the psychopaths in power want us to do), and just look around at each other—be with each other—you can see that we are not so divided; we are a tolerant, sensitive community.

If the system's making us sick, don't catalogue symptoms—throw a (metaphorical) brick. Aim at the gears, not the neighbours. Less sheen, more nerve; sharper notes, not nicer ones. Don't sand the edges—expose them. Point the camera at causes, make room for real critique, and work in the seams where the truth hides. Animation's field is absurdly wide—push it until something rattles.

CHAPTER 8

The Animation Pimp's Revised Guide to Festival Submissions

*O*VER 20 YEARS AGO, *I wrote a very snarky, very playful guide to submitting your film to festivals.*[1] *It was written in 2003, so it's a bit out of date. Let's try again for 2026.*

1. READ THE FESTIVAL RULES AND REGULATIONS. They are not novels. It will take you 5–10 minutes, and it will save you—and us—a hell of a lot of aggravation. I understand that not everyone speaks a festival's language, but there are excellent translation apps now. There's just no excuse.

2. Make the work you want to make. Don't do it for Mom and Dad, your teacher, or a studio. That will get you nowhere and leave you with a gaping pit of dissatisfaction. I've actually heard people say they think their film is an "OIAF film." I have no idea what that means. It's a bit insulting, frankly. You're assuming I have some fixed identity that never evolves. I've looked back at past OIAF competitions and scratched my head over a choice or two. That's a positive sign to me that I've changed since then.

DOI: 10.1201/9781003633181-9

IMAGE 8.1 The Animation Pimp Turns Hulk (drawing by Andreas Hykade)

3. If you have a distributor, it's your responsibility to know what they're doing with your film. I've heard many animators express surprise when their film ends up at a festival—or, conversely, doesn't get submitted. Recently, an animator was furious to discover that their film had been submitted to a state-funded Russian festival. I feel for them, but it's still on you to mind your work. It's your film, not the distributors' or the producers'.

4. Do your research about festivals. There are some scumbag outfits that are out for money and nothing more. Over the years, there have been stories of animators being ripped off. Don't be lazy. Don't fall into the thinking that you desperately need any festival's approval. That will only lead to bad choices.

5. Do not—and some filmmakers I'd label as acquaintances do this—text me to say your film has been submitted. It's my job to watch every submission. I know what you're trying to do, and it won't work. In fact, it can backfire. Just trust the process.

6. If your film is rejected, don't take it so hard. Selection is a highly subjective process (see what I wrote in Chapter 5). You have about a 5% chance of getting selected for the OIAF. In 2025, we received over 2,800 submissions. We generally accept around 100 films for Competition and Panorama. It's not easy to get in, but there are so many festivals now that you're likely to find a home. If not, well, then you need to ask yourself some hard questions about the work.

7. If your film is rejected, do not ask the festival to reconsider. It ain't gonna happen.

8. If your film is rejected, do not ask the festival to give you feedback. First, I know some animators who've bitched and moaned for decades about festivals not giving detailed feedback. Well, sorry, bud—that's not our job. Find a critic for that. Furthermore, do you honestly think I have time to write detailed reports on 2,800+ films? Second, as I've said elsewhere, I might pinpoint parts of a film that didn't appeal to me—but another programmer might love that exact thing. Just accept the decision and move on.

9. READ THE RULES! (Again.)

10. When a festival says "pick one category," that does not mean "pick three categories."

11. Make sure we can stream your submission. We don't do downloads. Who knows what demons lurk within those downloads, plus it slows down the process, making an already exhausting process all the more frustrating.

12. If you're a student, don't get ambitious—stick with the student category. You'll have your time.

13. A side note to distributors: READ THE RULES! It's your job. Submission = contract.

Thank you, and good luck.

NOTE

1 https://www.awn.com/animationworld/animation-pimp-how-avoid-pissing-me-or-ottawa-festival-entry-tips-aka-festival-rant-2

CHAPTER 9

A Salty Salute

A Mixtape of Shorts from 35 Years

TAPE 1

You've Got a Friend in Me (Peter Millard, 2024, UK)

Millard's polarizing chaos: sound, colour, pop-culture debris colliding in gleeful anti-animation. Some people call it nonsense; that's pretty much the point. It's funny, unserious, and unafraid to look stupid—exactly what the often self-important festival landscape needs.

Crossroads (Raimund Krumme, 1991, Germany)

Minimal figures, a shifting frame, and a man who can't seem to get anywhere. Beckett, Buster Keaton, and graphic clarity rolled into seven minutes.

Nighthawk (Špela Čadež, 2016, Slovenia/Croatia)

A drunk badger on a night drive sounds like a gag; instead, we get a nonjudgmental, tense, sad portrait of addiction. Čadež lets the character be pathetic and human at once.

We Lived in Grass (Andreas Hykade, 1995, Germany)

A boy raised on the brutal line, "All woman is whore and all man is soldier," briefly discovers tenderness and then torches it. Drawn raw and fast, it shows how inherited violence digs in and refuses to leave. Hard to believe this ferocious thing was a student film.

Solar Walk (Réka Bucsi, 2018, Denmark/Hungary)

DOI: 10.1201/9781003633181-10

IMAGE 9.1 We Can Make Music (drawing by Andreas Hykade)

A playful, drifting trip through space, creation, and abstract little beings. Bucsi makes cosmic stuff feel casual and musical instead of grandiose. It's the good kind of aimless.

We Eat Shit / We Drink Too Much (Chris Lavis & Maciek Szczerbowski, 2016–2017, Canada)

Everyone praises their big, lush films, but these tiny *Naked Island* shorts are my favourites: brutally concise, self-lacerating, and hilariously bleak.

Son of Satan (J.J. Villard, 2003, USA)

Looks like a messy sketchbook, sounds like a tape dub, hits like a punk song. A violent act by three boys spirals into doubt, guilt, and the realization that it all started at home. It's an ugly, honest little scream about how abuse and bullying keep recycling.

TAPE 2

Tower Bawher (Theodore Ushev, 2005, Canada)

Three weeks of constructivist fury set to Sviridov's *Time, Forward.* Lines and shapes build and collapse, suggesting grand projects—and their futility.

In a Pig's Eye (Atsushi Wada, 2010, Japan)

A family goes about its day while a gigantic pig sits right there. Deadpan absurdity about how we absorb strangeness and carry on. Wada's timing is so calm, it becomes funny.

Unity (Tobias Stretch, 2014, USA)

Life-size outdoor stop-motion: a dead man, three otherworldly figures, and a ritual of reclamation. Technically gorgeous and strangely uplifting.

Marcel, King of Tervuren (Tom Schroeder, 2013, USA/Belgium)

Based on a real rooster, told like a Greek tragedy. Loose, energetic painting style, rotoscoped bits, and an absurd voiceover about survival, betrayal, and mortality.

The Red Book (Janie Geiser, 1994, USA)

Dreamy, cut-out, noirish exploration of memory and language from the viewpoint of a woman with amnesia. Delicate, mysterious, very Geiser.

1895 (Priit Pärn & Janno Põldma, 1995, Estonia)

Pärn uses cinema's centenary to mock cinema itself. A faux-Lumière travels through exaggerated national stereotypes while Pärn reminds us film has shaped—and faked—our ideas of history, identity, even memory. Dense, rude, referential, and totally alive. An anti-cinema salute made by someone gleefully complicit.

TAPE 3

Feeling My Way (Jonathan Hodgson, 1997, UK)

On paper it's just a walk, but Hodgson turns it into a map of the restless mind—memories, judgements, ambient sound, tiny observations all brushing past each other. It's a perfect portrait of consciousness in motion.

Revolver (Filmtecknarna, 1993, Sweden)

A series of looping domestic images—fish kneading, faces flipping, weddings revolving—tied together by rhythm. Feels like a dream about family life made by the Fleischers after a long night on mushrooms.

Hilary (Anthony Hodgson, 1995, UK)

Technically scruffy but emotionally precise. A father tells his daughter about Hilary—a feckless woman, maybe her mother, maybe her future—over Satie-like piano. The dialogue has that Hal Hartley dryness, and the whole thing floats somewhere between bedtime story and regret.

The Datum Point (Ryo Orikasa, 2015, Japan)

A calm, clay-and-ink meditation on sea, motion, and constant change. It's the kind of film you feel more than analyze—like a small cinematic meditation session.

At the Quinte Hotel (Bruce Alcock, 2005, Canada)

Al Purdy's poem turned into a mixed-media barroom whirl—flowers, beer, fistfights, tenderness, and the sad truth that poetry doesn't pay for drinks.

Carnival of Animals (Michaela Pavlátová, 2006, Czech Republic)

Pavlátová turns Saint-Saëns into a celebration of sex, desire, awkwardness, and fantasy. Bodies distort, play, collide. It's funny and shameless and reminds you animation can handle eroticism better than live action.

Bird in the Window (Igor Kovalyov, 1996, USA)

A man returns to a house that's familiar and alien; a child keeps trying to reach him; memory and guilt won't line up. It's as mysterious and emotionally loaded as anything in Kovalyov's trilogy.

Impossible Figures and Other Stories II (Marta Pajek, 2016, Poland)

A woman wanders an impossible, empty house while Michelle Gurevich's song haunts the soundtrack. Bleached drawings, precise timing, and a quiet push toward self-awareness.

Lesley the Pony Has an A+ Day! (Christian Larrave, 2014, USA)

Sugar-coated, hyper-violent, kid-brain chaos. It nails that surreal, too-much energy of children's drawings and makes it actually funny.

TAPE 4

Who I Am and What I Want (Chris Shepherd & David Shrigley, 2005, UK)

Shrigley's dumb-smart drawings plus Kevin Eldon's machine-gun narration equal a hilariously miserable portrait of a man coming apart. It keeps Shrigley's book energy but actually becomes cinema—fast, sharp, and perfectly voiced.

Please Say Something (David OReilly, 2009, Ireland/Germany)

A futuristic cat and mouse love story, told with lo-fi aesthetics.

Funny, cold, and unexpectedly moving about miscommunication.

Crossing the Stream (Skip Battaglia, 2006, USA)

A man leads his horse across a stream—drawn, scraped, sounded so precisely it becomes spiritual. A small film that feels big.

Franz Kafka's A Country Doctor (Kōji Yamamura, 2007, Japan)

Kafka's story of a burned-out doctor turned into a painterly fever dream—bodies stretching, space warping, accusations everywhere. One of the best literary adaptations in animation.

Altair (Lewis Klahr, 1994, USA)

Collage noir built from the 1940s magazines, looping to music. Desire, booze, longing, and the endless itch to be the brightest star in the room.

Flux (Chris Hinton, 2002, Canada)

Miró-like scribbles and smudges bouncing through birth, family, ageing, death. Rough, rhythmic, funny, and somehow tender.

Little Cow (Igor Lazin, 2001, Hungary)

A cow sits in a tree and sings about sitting in a tree. That's literally it, and it's delightful. If this doesn't make you grin, slap yourself before I do.

TAPE 5

Jukebox (Run Wrake, 1995, UK)

A collagey, beat-heavy stream of consciousness—Curtis Mayfield, meathead figures, pop-icons-on-repeat. Watching it feels like being stuck in a club and a dream at the same time.

The Hat (Michèle Cournoyer, 2001, Canada)

One seamless chain of metamorphoses about sex, abuse, and performance. An exotic dancer remembers childhood trauma while bodies, objects, and hats morph in and out of each other. It's erotic, upsetting, and beautifully controlled.

Erodium Thunk (Winston Hacking, 2017, Canada)

A collage dive into half-remembered 1970s/1980s ads: comforting images torn, interrupted, reassembled. Feels like wandering through someone else's VHS childhood, sweet and a bit sinister.

Yoriko Mizushiri (Futon) (2012, Japan)

Soft colours, thin lines, slow pacing—sensual animation about bodies, bedding, and food. Nothing rushed, nothing overexplained. She invites you to feel, not decode.

The Sound of Music (Phil Mulloy, 1993, UK)

Mulloy's bleak city of violence, hypocrisy, and gluttony, seen by a jazz musician who's running out of patience. It's funny in that Mulloy way—because everything is awful and we're complicit.

Git Gob (Philip Eddolls, 2009, Canada)

Two odd creatures encounter a hole and argue about it. Perfectly timed, perfectly dumb, over in a blink. Sometimes that's all you need.

Teat Beat of Sex (Signe Baumane, 2008, USA/Latvia)

Short, raunchy, funny monologues about sex from a woman who refuses to be coy. She lets female desire be loud, messy, and smart.

The Wrong Trousers (Nick Park, 1993, UK)

Yes, it's popular. It's also perfectly structured, funny, and has the greatest penguin villain in cinema. A reminder that commercial doesn't mean dull.

Beavis and Butt-Head: "Animation Sucks" (Mike Judge, 1995, USA)

A teacher rhapsodizes about the beauty of movement, while Beavis and Butt-Head sit motionless. It's a perfect, stupid little jab at animation's tendency to take itself too seriously.

CHAPTER 10

Bonus Track

MOST ATTENDEES HAVE NO clue about the sacrifices behind a festival. Kelly—who's made more sacrifices for the OIAF than anyone—will tell you a summer holiday is basically impossible. In September, 12-hour days are standard. Will we have enough sponsorship? Government funding? Entries? Ticket sales? Will our employment-programme staff bail right before the event? There's a reason "event organizer" ranks among the most stressful jobs. And yet it's still exhilarating to watch people come together and see great films. Festivals are transformative. They're worth it.

—

Despite the personal dramas and mini-dramas, I'm never not grateful for the life this festival world gave me. I used to feel like a fraud, like I'd lucked into a job I wasn't qualified for. Maybe I did. But I squeezed the chance for all it was worth and built a pretty decent career.

When the recognition started coming, I felt embarrassed—and also amused. I somehow picked up two "lifetime-ish" nods while still alive and unqualified: in 2020, the Animafest Zagreb Award for Outstanding Contribution to Animation Studies, and in 2022, the Prix René Jodoin for contributions to Canadian animation. Is it success or an administrative screw-up? Groucho Marx still whispers in my ear about not joining any club that would have me as a member. Thirty-five years on, that spark of defiance is a shade dimmer, but it's still there.

—

This book fought me. I've always mixed fact and fiction and shown the mess, but seeing the whole forest at once was rough. Some will call it

DOI: 10.1201/9781003633181-11

IMAGE 10.1 Early draft of OIAF04 poster by Andreas Hykade

TMI. Fine. I can't demand honesty from filmmakers, programmers, and organizers and then hand you something airbrushed. I'm not an island; the work sits beside a lot of questionable choices. Pretending otherwise would be a lie. If any of this helps—if it loosens a little stigma—good. We're flawed and scriptless. We learn on the fly. I feel shame and regret; I also feel stubborn about strutting forward, stumbling forward, learning in fragments. I'll screw up again. So will you. Knowing that we will means we're not alone.

IMAGE 10.2 As we go up we go down

Bibliography

BOOKS — ANIMATION

Robinson, Chris. *Unsung Heroes of Animation*. John Libbey, 2005.

Robinson, Chris. *Estonian Animation: Between Genius and Utter Illiteracy*. John Libbey, 2007.

Robinson, Chris. *The Animation Pimp*. AWN Press, 2007.

Robinson, Chris. *Canadian Animation: Looking for a Place to Happen*. John Libbey, 2008.

Robinson, Chris. *Animators Unearthed: A Guide to the Best of Contemporary Animation*. Continuum, 2010.

Robinson, Chris. *Japanese Animation: Time Out of Mind*. John Libbey, 2010.

Robinson, Chris. *Mad Eyed Misfits: Writings on Indie Animation*. CRC Press, 2022.

Robinson, Chris. *Cheer and Loathing: Scattered Ramblings on Indie Animation*. CRC Press, 2023.

Robinson, Chris. *Earmarked for Collision: A Highly Biased Tour of Collage Animation*. CRC Press, 2024.

Robinson, Chris. *Dreaming a Way (of) Life: The Films of Lewis Klahr*. CRC Press, 2025.

Robinson, Chris. *Raw Outrage: The Films of Phil Mulloy*. CRC Press, 2025.

BOOKS — NON-ANIMATION

Robinson, Chris. *Ottawa Senators: Great Stories from the NHL's First Dynasty*. James Lorimer & Company, 2004. (reissued 2013)

Robinson, Chris. *Great Left Wingers: Stars of Hockey's Golden Age*. James Lorimer & Company, 2006.

Robinson, Chris. *Stole This from a Hockey Card: A Philosophy of Hockey, Doug Harvey, Identity & Booze*. Nightwood Editions, 2005.

Robinson, Chris. *Maurice Richard: The Most Amazing Hockey Player Ever*. James Lorimer & Company, 2011.

Robinson, Chris. *Love. Simple*. Amazon KDP, 2021.

GRAPHIC / ILLUSTRATED MEMOIR

Robinson, Chris, with illustrations by Andreas Hykade. *My Balls Are Killing Me*. Amazon KDP, n.d. Serialized in *Galaxy Brain Magazine*.

SCREENWRITING

Lipsett Diaries. Directed by Theodore Ushev, written by Chris Robinson, National Film Board of Canada, 2010.

Index

For Product Safety Concerns and Information please contact our EU
representative GPSR@taylorandfrancis.com
Taylor & Francis Verlag GmbH, Kaufingerstraße 24, 80331 München, Germany

www.ingramcontent.com/pod-product-compliance
Ingram Content Group UK Ltd.
Pitfield, Milton Keynes, MK11 3LW, UK
UKHW022121190926
475702UK00013B/1567
* 9 7 8 1 0 4 1 0 5 9 6 6 0 *